POPULAR
PARRAKEETS

POPULAR PARRAKEETS

Australasian and Asian Species in Aviculture

Dulcie and Freddie Cooke

Photographs by Cyril Laubscher

CASSELL

LONDON · NEW YORK · SYDNEY

First published in the UK 1989 by **Blandford Press**
An imprint of Cassell
Artillery House, Artillery Row, London SW1P 1RT

Text copyright © Dulcie and Freddie Cooke 1989
Photographs copyright © Cyril Laubscher 1989

Distributed in the United States by
Sterling Publishing Co, Inc,
2 Park Avenue, New York, NY 10016

Distributed in Australia by
Capricorn Link (Australia) Pty Ltd
PO Box 665, Lane Cove, NSW 2066

British Library Cataloguing in Publication Data

Cooke, Dulcie
  Popular parrakeets.
  1. Pets : Parrakeets. Care – Manuals
  I. Title   II. Cooke, Freddie
  636.6'865

ISBN 0 7137 2028 X

Typeset by Inforum Ltd, Portsmouth
Printed and bound in Great Britain by
Biddles Ltd, Guildford and King's Lynn

Contents

Acknowledgements

Freddie and I wish to thank Alan Jones B. Vet.Med., MRCVS for the very valuable contribution he has made with the chapter on avian diseases, their treatment and prevention.

Our special thanks go to Cyril Laubscher for making the photography of the birds in this book a work of art.

We also thank wildlife artist Steve Lings for his beautifully executed sketches and drawings.

Thanks are also due to our family and many friends for being so patient with us during the writing of this book, and especially we wish to thank the many aviculturists who have allowed us to view their collections.

Our grateful thanks go to Mrs Thelma Batchelor for producing a beautifully typed manuscript out of our respective handwriting.

DULCIE COOKE
Epsom, 1988

Freddie and I join Cyril in thanking the following aviculturists for their kind assistance in allowing their birds to be photographed for this book: Charles Attard; Marion & Andrew Cripps; Phil Dobinson; Ken & Shirley Epps; Rodney & Joan Hamilton; Lucien Horowitz; David James; Barry Kyme; Kath Kyme; Stanley Maughan; Mick O'Connell; Ron Oxley; Brian Pettit; Mick & Berl Plose; Stan & Jill Sindel; George Smith; Mick & Jean Uden; Frank Wagner.

Introduction

Of all the higher forms of life, birds are perhaps the most beautiful, the most musical in many cases, the most admired – and now, in many parts of the globe, the most defended. Without them much of our world would seem lifeless and silent. Those of us who have kept birds in aviaries all our lives know well the joy of watching birds go about their daily business, and the joy of being greeted by all of them (yes, *all* of them! when arriving home again after a long day's journey. We also know what it is to trudge through deep snow and struggle with frozen locks to feed and water our birds, and how very healthy we stay.

We know the joy of sitting in our garden on a summer's day, surrounded by birds, the wild blackbirds, thrushes, chaffinches, blue tits, and our own Turquoisines, Splendids, Cockatiels, and many others. They are all confiding, and all know they belong to a little community which provides contentment for them and endless joy and happiness for us, and, we believe, our many visitors and friends, too.

This book is written to help those who are newcomers to aviculture and also those who have some experience of keeping birds. In this second group will be people who perhaps feel they would like to venture towards new horizons and are seeking information about the management, feeding, housing and breeding of the more popular and easily obtainable parrakeets, which, in their wild state, live in Australia, New Zealand, the surrounding islands and in many parts of Asia.

Birds which have friendly natures, are aviary-bred, relatively inexpensive to buy, and easy to feed and house, are the desire of a great many people who care very much for birds, but have neither the time nor the financial resources of some of the world's most dedicated aviculturists.

The term 'parrakeets' is used to describe certain species which, in some books, may be described as parrots. Only mainly seed-eating birds are included, and many hints are given which, it is

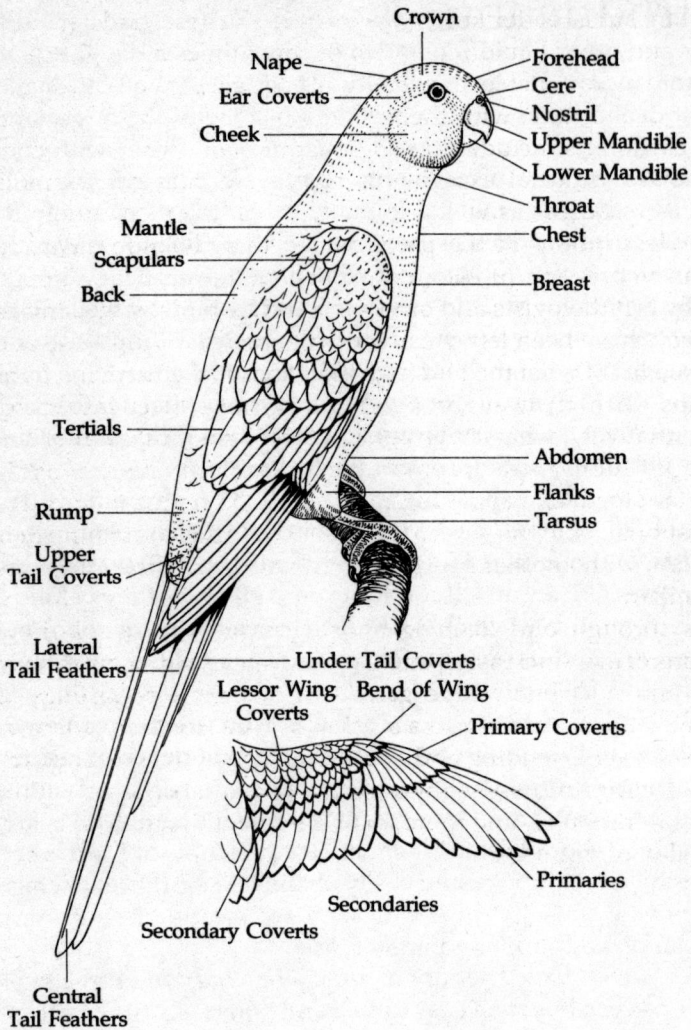

Fig. 1 External anatomy (topography) of parrakeet, plus vital wing detail.

hoped, should help readers to decide whether or not a certain species of bird would be the right choice for them. No Australian or Asian lories or lorikeeks are included. These birds require nectar and other liquid foods two or three times a day, and are therefore more suitable for avicultural specialists, who can spend a great deal of time with them. Nor are some of the larger and rarer parrakeets included, as these require an owner with considerable avicultural experience, not to mention considerable financial resources as well.

The descriptions of the parrakeets in this book are meant to give an impression of colour, size and character. Many terms, used by ornithologists and others to describe birds with 'clinical' accuracy, have been left out in favour of endeavouring to give a general idea of what the bird is going to look like when seen from perhaps 1 m (3 ft) away through two layers of protective netting; or, alternatively, what it will look like from 5 cm (2 in) away when taking favourite foods from the hand. We think this is what is important to many people embarking on the keeping of birds for the first time, or to those who feel they would like to enlarge their collection with another species of bird with which they may not be familiar.

It is through bird keeping and aviculture that whole new horizons of ever-increasing interest will appear, with new friends made and new knowledge gained in this most rewarding of pastimes. Aviculture is also a science, whose frontiers of knowledge are ever extending and enlarging. One of the great advantages of aviculture as a hobby is that there is total equality within this great fraternity, and there is always something new to learn, every day of one's life.

1
Housing

Both the positioning in the garden, and the selection of the right type of housing, are of the utmost importance. These factors will most certainly affect your success or lack of it in breeding the birds of your choice.

Flexibility is also important, as the minimum housing requirements suitable for the smaller parrakeets will not be suitable for larger species if a change is envisaged in the future. The biggest problem for the enthusiastic aviculturist is usually lack of space, so from the start it is best to allow for future additions to your collection by deliberately leaving space to extend or add houses and flights.

If you live in a built-up area and your aviaries have to be erected close to other properties, consideration should be given to the possible effect the keeping of birds could have on your neighbours. Some birds, like the Grass Parrakeets, are very quiet; most of the other birds we shall write about are tolerable – but not all! This aspect is very important and will be commented upon when the various species are discussed. Many people have obtained very colourful birds, which they have sited where they can be seen from inside their own house. Not having been informed about the possible noise factor when they acquired the birds, they have, unfortunately, subsequently had to part with them because their noise levels proved intolerable.

A factor to take into account when considering the type of aviary to have is the amount of time that can be given daily to feeding, cleaning up, etc. For the very busy, who only have spare time at weekends, a design giving ease of access, and which allows one to feed and water the birds quickly, probably in more than one aviary, is very important.

Most of the birds mentioned in this book will need sunshine during some part of the day, so choose a position where a fair amount of sun will reach into the flights at some period each day.

In the wild most of these birds come from dry open areas, not tropical forests, therefore placing the aviaries under very shady trees should be avoided.

An aviary, or aviaries, blended in to make a feature in a garden, can be most attractive and add to the general enjoyment of one's pastime.

Selecting an Aviary

First, it must be remembered that, due to the pugnacious nature of most of the parrakeet species, especially at breeding time, one pair only should be kept in an aviary. For this same reason, all adjacent flights between the birds should be double-wired. A further factor arises at breeding time, for often, if intending to go back to the nest for a second round, there is a limit to the length of time for which many parents will tolerate the young from the first nest. There will be no time then to decide what to do if tragedy is to be avoided, so an available spare aviary, or provision to section off an existing one, is required.

A large aviary, holding a number of attractive-looking birds, is not suitable for parrakeets: the choice will lie with a number of small aviaries, a bank of aviaries, or, more expensive, a large house with a number of built-in compartments, each with access for feeding and cleaning, and a common service walkway, with flights extending from each compartment on the outside of the house.

If a canary or budgerigar keeper wishes to change to parrakeet keeping, it is very likely that a large shed or building will already be available that can easily be adapted.

The illustrations on page 3 show some typical aviaries, but there are many variations, and if you intend to purchase one from a supplier or manufacturer, do not be in a hurry in making your choice. Competition is fierce, and designs and timber sizes vary greatly within a wide range of prices, so it is best first to obtain and compare all available literature. The weekly magazine *Cage and Aviary Birds* carries many advertisements, including second-hand bargains for the DIY enthusiast. Periodically, there are special issues covering housing and equipment.

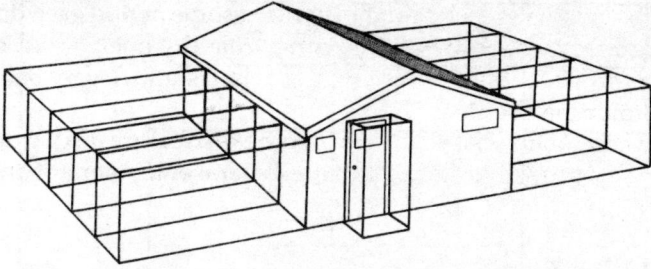

Fig.2 Span roof block of aviaries with entrance porch.

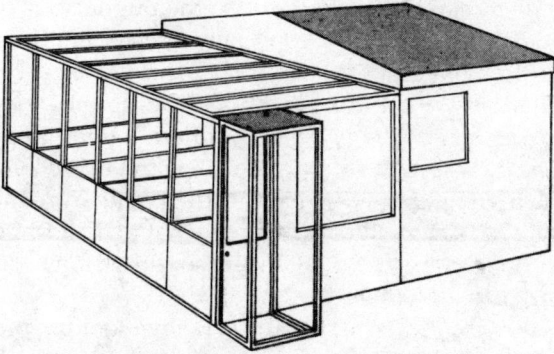

Fig.3 Block of six aviaries with entrance porch.

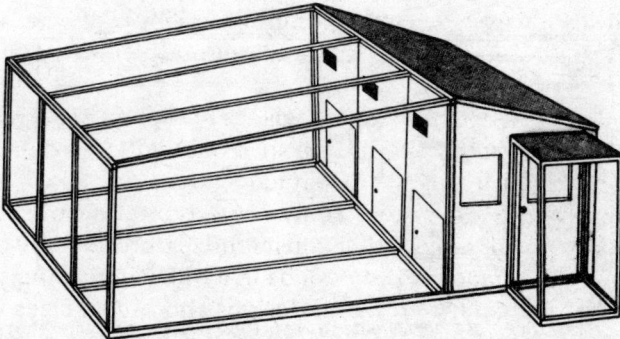

Fig.4 Aviaries for two pairs of birds, and one for their young, with entrance porch.

3

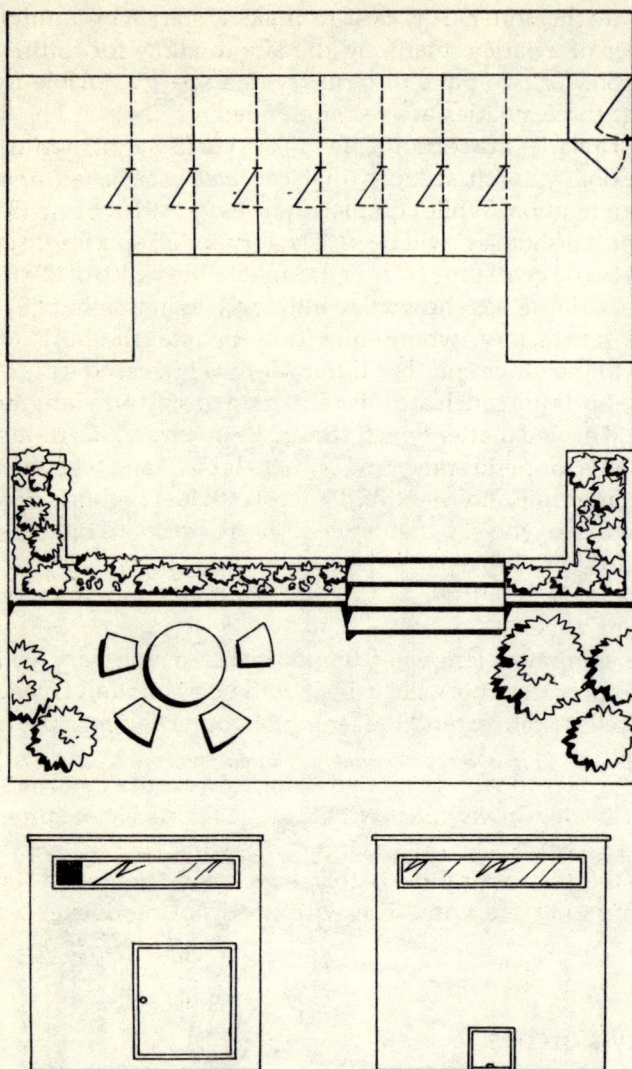

Fig. 5 Ornamental aviaries as a feature in a garden, with eight sections inside the house, six small flights, two large ones, and an entrance porch to the flights.

For the beginner, it is best to make a start with a minimum number of aviaries, planning the site to allow for future additions. So, for two pairs of birds, with a space available for any young, three aviaries are recommended.

Most aviaries are sectional, in 91 × 61 cm (3 × 6 ft) modules. Go for flexibility, with sections that can easily be taken apart for future alteration. While complete houses 91 × 91 × 61 cm (3 × 3 × 6 ft), or half-houses, will be satisfactory for all species discussed in this book, give some further thought to the width of the flights. Our experience has shown that although flight widths of 91 cm (3 ft) are satisfactory, when entered by people, the birds will fly down to the other end, but if the width is increased to 122 cm (4 ft), the birds are much steadier and tend to stay on a longitudinal perch. This is a matter which should be given serious thought by those able to spend some time with their birds and who like them to become tame and friendly. The cost of wider flights is minimal. Ignore those who say that tame birds are not good breeders. We have not found this to be the case in the many species we have kept, and, in fact, there are many advantages with tame birds at breeding time.

The minimum length of flights required will vary with the species of birds. This will be dealt with later, but don't forget you may well wish to extend the length of your aviaries in the course of time.

Always try to view before you buy, and ensure that the size of the twilweld, or wiremesh, fitted to the flights is not larger than 2.5 × 1.25 cm (1 × ½ in), as larger sizes would allow predators to reach the feet of any birds that have been frightened and are hanging onto the wire. The wire need not be thicker than 19 SWG.

Safety Porches

Proper provision must be made to ensure that birds cannot escape when the aviaries or flights are entered. In advertisements for aviaries, porches will seldom be shown or mentioned, although they are usually available as extras. Most aviaries, especially at the lower end of the price range, have low entrance doors, and one must bend down to enter. The theory here is that, as the door is entered, the birds will fly high and not escape. This is a fallacy. Every year many bird keepers, find, to their horror, that a bird, usually a favourite, will fly low and escape. When this does happen, it is unlikely that the bird will return, or even be found again.

Our experience has shown that a proper safety porch is a vital requirement, whether built into the design or added as an extra. This is particularly so with the smaller species of birds. Even with a safety porch, one must always watch the friendly, fast moving and fearless Kakarikis very carefully.

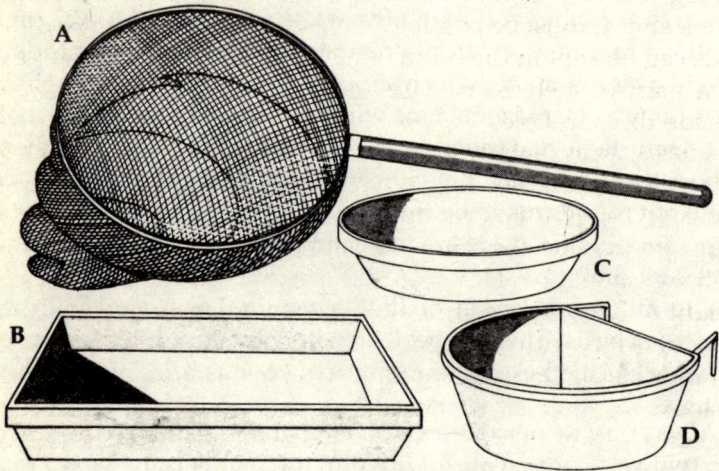

Fig.6 Equipment: **A** *catching net;* **B** *a water container large enough to allow bathing;* **C** *an earthenware bowl makes a good food container for either seed or soft food, and is easy to wash;* **D** *clip-on plastic food containers are useful as extra utensils for food in the flights at breeding time.*

The porch should have a full-sized door, which makes access easy, especially when carrying utensils, cages, boxes, etc. The door into the flight should also be full size. When it is necessary to catch up a bird, it is so much simpler, and less stressful to both birds and their owners, to catch them in the confines of a porch rather than have them dashing about in the flight. A porch of 91 sq cm (3 sq ft) is adequate for all birds. We usually incorporate a narrow shelf to hold seed trays and any other small items that are regularly taken in and out of the aviaries.

Aviaries for Grass Parrakeets

A common size of aviary is suitable for all the species. It is possible to keep them in a width of 75 cm (2 ft 6 in), but we would recommend at least 91 cm and, ideally, 122 cm (4 ft) to give the flexibility previously mentioned.

It is not necessary to have a full-sized house. A half-sized house of 91 cm (3 ft) high, 91–122 cm (3–4 ft) wide, and 61–91 cm (2–3 ft) deep is entirely satisfactory, and the cost is less. The front of a half-house should have a large door for access, which opens into the flight, with a window running along the top, and a pop hole at one end. It must be possible to close the pop hole, so that the birds can be kept in the house when required. They gain access from narrow shelves, which should be fitted both inside and outside the pop hole.

Houses are available with very small doors fitted on the back to give access for easy feeding, but in such cases a window will also be needed so that you can make sure that any birds inside the house go out into the flight before the door is opened.

Flights should be at least 1.8 m (6 ft) long. (The birds will enjoy a flight of 2.7 [9 ft] even more.) Starting with three aviaries, or a block of three, with a common entrance through a safety porch, communicating doors in the flights will be necessary. All flights adjacent to other birds must be double-wired, and, to avoid tragedies with cats or any other predators, we strongly recommend double-wiring throughout.

Protection against inclement weather is a must for all Grass Parrakeets, so roofs of flights should be covered with PVC or some similar sheeting. All these birds will seek out and sit in the sun. They can stand the cold, even severe cold, very well, but cannot tolerate draughts, wind, rain or damp conditions.

We cannot stress too strongly the advisability of complete protection during the winter months; especially for young Splendids. From November until April all our flights are fitted with detachable panels, made of clear, rigid PVC sheeting screwed to a light wooden framework. This keeps the birds very comfortable. Our oldest pair of Splendids, kept under these conditions in the cold area where we live, will soon be entering their eleventh breeding season.

We do not provide any heat but, to keep severe frosts from chilling the air from above when the birds are roosting, the roofs of the houses are insulated, using a layer of fibre glass held by plywood. This is very simple to fit and secure.

Birds can only remain in good condition by maintaining their body temperature. Being small birds, with a relatively low intake of food, Grass Parrakeets need to eat very frequently. Although they will fill their crops very full before the long winter nights, the period before daylight and the next meal is very long for small birds. It is possible that their stamina could thus be reduced, and the time then taken to regain good condition could delay the start of the breeding season. Therefore, if it is possible to fit electric light, this is a tremendous advantage. We keep lights on at a low level throughout the hours of darkness, which are just sufficient for the birds to be able to see to feed late into the night and in the early morning.

Aviaries for Kakarikis, Many Coloureds and Stanley Rosellas

Half-houses, similar to those suggested for Grass Parrakeets, are very satisfactory for these birds, but the width must be a minimum of 91 cm (3 ft). Once again, if cost and space can be afforded, a width of 122 cm (4 ft) is recommended. The flights must be at least 2.7 m (9 ft) long.

All these birds are very hardy and while not requiring the very closed-in winter protection needed by Grass Parrakeets, we always recommend lining the roofs of all houses. The roofs of the flights should be covered, and should all be double-wired. Protection should be given on bad-weather sides during the winter months.

Our experience has shown that when only a single brood is raised, the parents will quite happily tolerate their young. But, as with most other birds, they will not do so if going to the nest for a second time, so a spare aviary, or other suitable space, must be available to enable a rapid transfer when trouble arises.

Aviaries for Adelaides, Golden Mantleds, Green Mealies, Pennants (Crimson) and Yellow Rosellas, Rock Poplars, Blossom Heads and Plum Heads

Half-houses are as satisfactory for these larger birds as they are for the smaller species. Being less expensive than full-sized houses is not their only advantage; they are so much easier for feeding and cleaning. Both the width and depth of the houses should be a minimum of 91 cm (3 ft), but a width of 122 cm (4 ft) would be ideal. Flights should be at least 91 cm (3 ft) wide, but again we consider a width of 122 cm (4 ft) to be better. Be sure that adjoining flights are double-wired, even if a chance is taken with predators by not double-wiring the outsides.

Like their owners, birds appreciate comfort, so we recommend insulating the roofs and protecting the bad-weather sides of the flights during the winter. The birds will greatly benefit from this extra care, and it is very noticeable that, in the spring, they will come into breeding condition much more readily than birds kept in open and exposed conditions.

A spare aviary, or suitable space, should be available for the segregation of the young, as they may have to be parted from their parents in a hurry.

The possibility of woodwork chewing needs to be considered. It is usually only found to be a real problem with some Pennants. Aviaries constructed from metal are not a necessity, but, if the extent of the chewing does become a worry, protection can be given by fixing wire mesh, or thin metal strips, over the affected parts, and providing the offenders with some suitable branches to chew.

Aviaries for Alexandrines, Indian Ringnecks, Moustached Parrakeets and Princess of Wales

Of all the birds under discussion, these need the maximum amount of flight space that can be provided. A minimum length of 5.4 m (18 ft) is recommended; a width of 91 cm (3 ft) is satisfactory, but, as with the other birds, we would say 122 cm (4 ft) is better. Half-houses of 91 × 91 × 91 cm (3 × 3 × 3 ft) can be used. With Ringnecks, a greater width may be more satisfactory, as, out of the breeding season, many hens can be aggressive towards the cocks, so the more space they have, the better.

Good protection will be needed in the winter months, as the toes of Asian species can be badly affected by frostbite in very severe weather.

Alexandrines and Moustacheds always seem to like chewing at the woodwork, and, once started, this can be a problem to overcome. Anyone proposing to keep these particular birds should bear this in mind and be ready to protect any exposed woodwork in their aviaries.

Ringnecks, and most of the Asian species, go to the nest very early in the year, (in the UK this is usually in February). These birds breed freely and many people are very successful with them, but problems can arise if there is very cold weather at the time the eggs are laid. These birds will only breed at this time, so if you would really like to pamper your birds and alleviate any problems if breeding is intended, provide electricity. When wiring is installed for lighting the house, fit a junction box on the outside so that a separate supply and switch can be provided for heating a nestbox. It is vital that all wiring inside houses or flights be run in conduits and fitted to ensure that the birds cannot reach or chew at the live wires. The heated nestboxes are usually integrally made, with a 60-W bulb fitted underneath the base of the nest. The heated nestbox really comes to the fore when the breeding of expensive mutations is planned.

The Aviary Site

Careful planning is of the utmost importance. We have already mentioned consideration for neighbours, and the need for a reasonable amount of sunshine at some time of the day. Newcomers should see as many of the aviaries of other aviculturists as possible, to obtain ideas and avoid pitfalls. Buying the aviaries is a major expense: in the long run it will be less costly to get the position right first time, allowing for any additions or alterations that may be required in the future.

To be able to extend the length of flights is very important. At some time you may wish to keep birds of a larger species, and, while it is most likely that the size of the houses will be satisfactory, it is the length of the flights required which will decide what is possible.

Flights positioned where their length can be walked along by the keeper will not cause any problems with Grass Parrakeets, although there should be perches on the far side, so that, when approached, the birds can fly to the back. For the Rosellas and larger birds, this aspect can be a problem, as many will want to fly well away, especially if they are not visited very often. Years ago we had difficulty in trying to breed some Rosellas. The problem was overcome immediately the birds were moved to aviaries where the keeper walked along the end of the flights; the nest-boxes being positioned at the far end.

If an aviary is to be erected by an adjoining fence, make sure the distance any building can be erected from the fence is not specified by a local by-law. If it is to be approached by ground that could be churned up in wet weather, plan for a path or stepping stones to be laid. Paving stones, available in many sizes at garden centres, are very good for this purpose, as they are easy to move, should the layout be altered later.

Preparing the Site for Erection

If a full-sized house is to be used, whether it has a floor or not, it should be positioned and secured on a concrete base. A depth of 15 cm (6 in) is recommended, using four parts of coarse sand or fine gravel to one part of cement, laid on a foundation of rubble. It should be well above ground level to avoid pools of water lying on the ground. There must be no dampness in the houses; especially for Grass Parrakeets. A damp course can be made by laying a pliable sheet of plastic after the first 7.5 cm (3 in) of concrete have been laid.

To make certain that vermin cannot enter through the base, lay fine wire mesh over the rubble foundation before laying the concrete. If the house does not have a floor and rests directly on the base, take extra care when making the shuttering to take the concrete, and allow for the house to overlap very slightly on all sides, so that rainwater will not run underneath.

Grass or gravel is not considered satisfactory for the bases of flights. This sort of surface can harbour worms, the prevalence of which is very much underestimated in parrot-like birds. A lot of work is entailed in keeping such flights clean, and it will not be long before they will become so fouled as to need digging out and replacing.

We recommend paving stones as the most suitable base; being available in so many sizes, they are easy to handle and fit into a variety of flight shapes. Levelling is not difficult if they are set in sand and water will run away through the joints, which are too small to allow the entry of vermin. When laying, leave them at least 5 cm (2 in) wider than the flights, which can then be secured to the paving using rawlplugs and plated screws, to ensure that they are not blown over in high winds.

When half-houses are used, a concrete base is not required, and the whole aviary can be postioned on a flat bed of paving stones. Again, leave them protruding slightly around the whole area, to enable the bases of the panels to be fixed securely to the ground.

Erecting the Aviary
With a carefully prepared base, erection should be straightforward, but do use screws that have been treated to prevent rust, and galvanized nails, and paint over the ends of bolts and nuts after assembly. This small attention to detail will make the difference to the amount of work involved in any future alterations. Fix the aviary to the base using rawlplugs and plated screws.

When covering the flights, use screws and plastic cups, but before fitting the cover, consider the direction in which rainwater is required to run off. Normally, the roof of the house will slope from front to back, so if the run-off from the flight is required in this direction, the flight roof panels must be fixed higher at the front. To achieve this, a batten may have to be fitted along the top at the front of the house.

The size of the batten should allow the roof panel to extend over the top of the house. A further batten must then be fitted along the front of the flights. A steep slope is not necessary, as little as 5 cm (2 in) higher at the front will ensure that water will run to the rear.

Using plastic spacers, often supplied with screws and plastic cups, and longer screws as required, ensures that there will be no sag in the panels. If, for ease of feeding, a small door is fitted to the back of the house, a gutter will be required.

Preservatives
We protect the interiors of houses by applying a coat of white primer-sealer paint. This is not strictly necessary, but it does give more light and is easy to keep clean by applying further coats when required. For interior or exterior woodwork, do not use creosote; it is toxic to birds, takes a long time to dry, and has been known to be fatal if deposited in any quantity on a bird's feathers. Cuprinol is satisfactory, although much more expensive in the short term. Bio-Woody is excellent, causes no damage to birds or plants, is available in a range of colours, and is quick drying and non-fading.

The flight wiring, being galvanized, does not really need further protection, but it is unsightly and, most important, it is difficult for you to see the birds, clearly, and equally difficult for them to see out. This can be overcome by brushing or rolling a coat of black bitumastic paint onto both sides of the wire. Do not forget to paint the wire *before* double-wiring!

Finishing the Aviary
Food should be given inside the houses, so, if a full-sized house is used, a tray or shelf to take the receptacles should be fitted inside. Make this as large as possible, allowing sufficient space for the birds to fly up from the floor.

Half-houses are much easier to manage, as the food containers are placed directly on the high floor. For those whose time is limited, a small access door at the back, which avoids having to come through the flight, speeds up the feeding programme.

A perch should be fitted across the house near the back. It is important that this is positioned higher than any other perch in the flight, as the birds will normally go to roost in the highest possible position.

The sizes of the perches should range from 1.25 cm (½ in) diameter for Grass Parrakeets, 1.6 cm (5 in) diameter, for Rosellas, to 2.5 cm (1 in) diameter for Ringnecks. As has been said before, we do not favour long narrow flights with a perch at each end. We abandoned these years ago, as our experience showed that there is more flying activity in wide flights. In wider flights a variety of perches can be fitted along the length and at the ends. Different diameters should be used so that feet can be well exercised. Be sure that all perches are firmly and rigidly fixed to avoid the possibility of fertilization problems at mating time.

Branches of hazel, beech or willow can be introduced; the birds will enjoy these, and, very often, keeping the birds busy avoids the problem of feather plucking.

To minimise frostbite, make sure that your birds roost on perches of a large enough diameter so that the body feathers can cover the feet. On small perches the feet wil be very exposed and this can cause problems. Do get your birds inside their houses during the winter months. It takes very little time to teach them that they must go in when told. It will help if you fit shelves both on the outside and the inside of the pop holes. It must be possible to close the pop holes.

A convenient way of securing cuttlefish-bone, apple, carrot, etc., is to insert two headless nails, approximately 2.5 cm (1 in) apart, into an upright by a perch, or directly into a perch, leaving 2.5 cm (1 in) extended. Greenfood can be attached to the perches by twisting thin pieces of wire over it.

If electricity can be made available, it is both beneficial and useful; a dimmed light throughout the hours or darkness will enable the birds to get back to their perches if disturbed, and, as has been recommended for Grass Parrakeets, extends the feeding time.

A wide range of controllers, dimmers, time-switches, etc., is available, but be sure to employ a qualified electrician if you do not understand electricity. Security should be borne in mind; always fit strong padlocks. If electricity is installed, a whole variety of alarms can be fitted. One good, and not too expensive, type of deterrent is an infra-red floodlight, switched on by bodyheat as an intruder approaches.

Some Hints if the Aviary is Home-made

With costs continually rising, timber is very expensive, so, to be able to cut economically and avoid a seemingly endless waste of effort, it is suggested that a standard cross-sectional size is used for all structural timbers of both houses and flights. It is not a good idea to skimp on size. Structural timber 3.75 cm square (1 ½ in) and 1.6 cm (⅝ in) thick, tongued and grooved, for the cladding, is not only easy to work with, but gives the best final results.

The House

Make the framework in separate sections; front, back, sides and roof, including internal frames for doors, windows and pop-hole. Bolting the frames together with coachbolts is recommended. To achieve this before cladding the sections, drill holes for the bolts in one mating face only of the uprights. Drilling through when the sections are assembled avoids misalignments. To safeguard against the houses being blown over in gale-force wind, they should be fixed to the base, and at least two base members should be drilled for screws to be inserted in rawlplugs. These holes can then be used for marking the position of the rawlplugs in the concrete base. The house will, of course, have to be moved aside to allow for the drilling and fitting of the plugs. As an alternative, angle-iron posts, made to support chain-link fencing, can be well driven into the ground and secured to structural members with plated screws. It is always best to use only galvanized nails, and screws that have been treated to prevent rust. When making the roof, be sure to allow for the correct amount of overhang if a gutter is to be fitted.

Flight Panels

When marking out and cutting the framework, allow for the short ends to be positioned outside the long timbers to give better support for the roof panels. After cutting to length, pre-drill one upright only for attachment bolts, and drill one hole in the middle of the base timber to take a screw for anchoring to a rawlplug to be fitted in the floor. Drill holes for attachment bolts in the roofpanel framework. To avoid the timber splitting when joining the framework together, drill two slightly undersized holes to take the nails in one mating surface only, and mark the position of these holes by using an offcut of the timber being used. Treat all woodwork before fitting the wire. Mark the panels before fitting the wire. This will enable easy identification of the sides on which the wire is to be fitted (always on the inside of flights) and their position on erection.

For the wire screen, use only material that has been galvanized, and do not use a large size of mesh which would allow vermin to enter. Twilweld or weldmesh of 19 SWG, 2.5 × 1.25 cm (1 × ½ in) will be satisfactory for all species of birds mentioned. To ensure that the wire is not loose or floppy on the framework, staple it in position on one side and one end only, inserting the staples on the other sides pointing outwards, at an angle that will make the mesh taut. If positioning with a power-operated stapler, careful positioning by hand with a few staples first will give the same result.

Blacken the wire with bitumastic paint. Mesh panels for double-wiring, which are to be fitted to the outside of the flights after erection, should be painted on both sides before being fitted.

2
General Management and Hygiene

A great deal can be learnt about hygiene from watching wild birds at breeding time and also from watching the inherited traits of some domesticated species of birds. Country dwellers, and those with gardens containing one of the alpine or creeping varieties of thyme, a strongly perfumed herb, will have noticed blackbirds, thrushes, starlings, sparrows and others all tugging furiously at the extremely tough strands of this plant, spread out, as it often is, over patio stonework. The reason for this is that it acts as a powerful deterrent to mosquitoes, gnats and other insects.

Most of us have seen wild birds diligently removing droppings from a nest of young, either in the wild or on television. Some of us will have noted the look of disdain on a large parrot's face if the owner dares to offer a morsel which has been dropped on the floor. That bit is dirty, it has been dropped, it is no longer eatable, no matter how nice it might have tasted before.

So many problems can be avoided in aviculture by a little work done on a *regular* basis. A regular scrape and brush up of the house and flight once a week, ideally in the summer once a day, is preferable to a tremendous 'spring-clean' twice a year.

It is important to remember that whereas healthy excreta is relatively harmless as long as it is absolutely dry, it becomes a breeding ground for germs once it becomes damp. Therefore, if the owner is going to rely on hosing down aviary flights, the job has to be done very thoroughly. This would not be a good way to deal with the interiors of houses. In the climatic conditions experienced for so much of the year in the UK and many other parts of Europe, it would simply lead to a state of cold, damp misery for the birds.

Houses are best scraped and brushed, followed by a thorough spray with a good disinfectant made specially for birds. One such is Duramitex, obtainable from pet shops. Half a teaspoon to ½ litre (1 pt) of water, sprayed lightly around the house, should keep red mites away.

Another excellent deterrent for many insects is Banmite. This can be sprayed onto all surfaces of the house and lasts a long time.

If an infectious disease has attacked any of the birds, it might be necessary to remove them all to another place and use a blow-lamp on all woodwork perches, shelves, etc. In the case of an illness which is diagnosed as infectious by a veterinary practitioner, he or she should be asked to advise on the best way to make the aviary concerned safe for the remaining or future birds.

Nestboxes

Small nestboxes, used by Grass Parrakeets, Stanley Rosellas, Redrumps, Kakarikis, etc., are best taken down at the end of each breeding season and soaked for 48 hours in a clean dustbin filled with water and a liberal dash of any strong disinfectant, such as Parozone. The boxes must be thoroughly rinsed when taken out, then dried and stored in a warm dry place ready for the next breeding season.

Fig.7 Left: *nest box for Grass Parrakeets*; right: *nest box for medium-sized parrakeets, showing internal ladders.*

Many years ago one was constantly urged to make the nest-boxes for every conceivable species damp; some people even recommended making them quite wet at the base. Now the thinking is completely different. A report by Dr J. Baker BVSc, PhD, on nestbox humidity, carried out for the Lancashire, Cheshire and North Wales Budgerigar Society, states that 'using damp material in a nest box is usually unnecessary and also unwise, as if the nest is damp when the hen moves off, evaporation of large amounts of water could take place, causing the eggs to chill. . . . A damp nest box is also ideal for germs to live in and multiply.'

Nestboxes for the larger species of parrakeets discussed in this book will need to be cleared of all nesting material at the end of the breeding season, and cleaned out as much as possible. I give these big boxes a thorough spray with a good disinfectant, made specially for birds, at this time of year. Some breeders may feel it wise to block the nest entrance with a piece of plywood, to ensure that the hens do not get any ideas of late nesting into their heads.

With most of the larger species it is sufficient to clear the nest out. The hens then know 'that's that' for the year in question! Early nesters, like the Asian species, will need their nesting material renewed in plenty of time. Bigger birds tend to spend a lot of time in getting their home as they want it, weeks, even months, before they actually lay eggs.

Worming

The great importance of worming *all* parrot-type birds is much more generally realised now than it was a few years ago. However, still, year in, year out, we meet newcomers to bird keeping, and many experienced breeders, too, who cannot bring themselves to worm their birds individually. They think that putting a worming medicine in the drinking water will do the job satisfactorily. Certainly it is better than not worming the birds at all. Harkers produce a good medicine for this method, which can be bought at many pet shops and commercial bird establishments.

Unfortunately, most Australian birds, and some others, can go for long periods without water (even though they may suffer) and even if they do drink a prepared solution, they may not drink enough to kill off any worms *and their eggs* which they may be carrying. Far the best way to ensure the health of one's birds is to learn how to worm them individually. It really is not difficult; it just requires a little quiet, steady concentration. Birds are like animals; they quickly guess when someone is unused to administering medicine, and will play up most terribly at first. Confidence, on the part of the person doing the worming, comes with practice.

One of the very best worming treatments available now in the UK is Panacur. It is the Panacur 2.5 suspension sheep wormer *without additives* which should be obtained from a veterinarian. Not all vets are co-operative in this respect, and not all of them realise that this medicine has a 'life' of only *one year after the container is opened*. If the bird keeper does not meet with co-operation from his or her vet on this matter, the answer is simple, keep trying until a vet is found who knows enough about birds to understand that this medicine is necessary. The containers are quite large and expensive, but usually a veterinarian can be found who is already using this medicine for other animals, and will be able to supply a small amount. It should be kept in a cool dark place, not a refrigerator. It has a considerable sediment, so must be shaken before use.

We have used this medicine for some years on all our birds, and now give a much stronger dose than in years gone by. It is an excellent medicine, strong, but safe, and works by killing all worms and their eggs within the bird's body. They are then expelled, dead, over a period of about ten days.

To make an easy -to-give dose, put one part of Panacur (2.5 solution sheep wormer *without additives*) into five parts of water in a screw-top bottle, shake thoroughly and put the required dose into a syringe with, if possible, a 'reserve' dose in another syringe in case a lot is wasted as it is given. To newcomers, and those unused to worming birds, we would say do not try to use a catheter, or even a hard rubber tube attached to the nozzle of a syringe. Large birds will bite through the latter in seconds and possibly swallow it, perhaps with lethal results, and small birds, such as Grass Parrakeets, could possibly have their delicate little throats irreparably damaged by a tube being inserted.

The best method, until one has gained quite a lot of experience, is simply to use the nozzle of the syringe in either side of the bird's mouth. We use a 5- or 10-ml syringe with the hypodermic needle removed. If the bird is medium-sized or larger, hold it in a gloved hand and allow it to place its feet on your chest; this gives it confidence. If possible, get the first finger of the 'holding' hand over the top of the bird's head and let it bite on the glove. This opens its mouth, and it will then be possible to slip the nozzle of the syringe into the side of the mouth and press home the plunger. Some of the medicine is almost bound to be lost, so give a little more, if necessary. Sometimes the medicine, or some of it, goes down the throat too fast, causing it to come back through the nostrils. This will not harm the bird, nor will it be harmed if some gets into its eyes. If it is a lot, rinse them with clear water, but a little can be dispersed by very gently smoothing the closed eye of the bird. If the bird is quite large, and the owner unused to worming, it may be advisable to have a helper, one to hold the bird in gloved hands, the other to give the medicine; but always be sure to allow the bird to put its feet on something, as this tends to stop any panicking on the part of the bird.

Breeders who have experience of worming may prefer to use a tube for birds the size of, say, Stanley Rosellas. For this size of bird we fit a very small electrical cable onto the syringe, called a single-core multi-strand. It would be best to take the syringe to an electrical supplier to get the right size. The cable has to be soaked in hot water to make it soft; having first carefully removed all the wires. When it is soft, pull one end over the nozzle of the syringe, far enough to make it secure, then cut the cable to about 3.75 cm (1 ½ in) in length, and file the end to make it absolutely smooth. Bend it very slightly, so that it will go down a bird's throat more easily. I never insert these tubes more than about 2 cm (¾ in) and, as stated above, it is *never* used for Grass Parrakeets or large birds.

When using a tube, it must be guided from the front of the mouth straight over the tongue and down the throat. It will be found that the bird understandably contracts its muscles and appears to 'close' its throat. Patience, plus talking and whistling, will help to relax the bird. It is best to give worming medicine on a fairly full stomach, for example in the morning after the birds have had a good feed. Using Panacur, worms and eggs will be expelled dead over a period of up to 10 days. This means that there is no likelihood of the bird dying as a result of the worming medicine having causing many worms to be expelled all at once, which can cause a fatal blockage of the intestines. This did happen with some types of worming medicine which were commonly used in the past.

Rodents and other predators

Stoats and Weasels
These are only likely to be encountered in country districts, and even then they will only cause trouble if they can gain easy access to an aviary, for example, via a drain pipe. They have been known to get into aviaries this way and kill large birds.

Rats
Rats should certainly not be a problem if the advice given about aviary foundations in the chapter on housing is followed. Rats are only likely to be a problem where domestic fowls or ducks are kept, and if food is left lying on the ground. Probably the best way to deal with these rodents is by poisoning, but the *greatest possible care* must be exercised in this respect. The poison *must* be covered over completely, so that wild birds cannot get at it and possibly carry it to places where it can be picked up by cats and dogs, etc.

Mice
House mice and their pretty little relatives, the field mice, can be a problem because they can squeeze through such tiny holes, especially when very young. The excreta of mice is not so harmful to birds, but mouse urine on seed, etc., can and does kill them.

Humane mouse traps (little boxes which can be kept in an aviary) are the best way to deal with this problem. They are very effective if left for some time, as both mice and birds become used to them. The mice are, of course, caught alive, so a trip into a country area where they can be let out is probably the best way to dispose of them. Large birds, especially, are not really scared of mice. We once had one breeding pair of quite large parrakeets who used to throw bits of food onto the floor every day. We only found out why when a very fat field mouse was unable to follow her family back out through the double wire. We transported her to a nearby wood, where she probably lived quite happily.

Foxes

Urban and other foxes can frighten birds very badly, especially during the summer months, when the birds are breeding in the flights. One pair of Princess of Wales Parrakeets we had never did breed one season because every time a fox came into the garden, the cock 'shouted' and the hen rushed out to see what the matter was.

Foxes breed early, and by January one can hear the quick yap, yap, yap of the young ones calling to the vixen. This is very disturbing for early breeders like Ringnecks. Probably the best deterrent for this problem is a large strong dog or, better still, two dogs. The birds and the dogs will become totally used to each other within days. Any reasonably trained dog will learn very quickly to leave his or her birds alone, and to guard them carefully.

Insects

It is often not realised that those little gnats and mosquitoes, apparently harmlessly gyrating over the compost heap, or over that pretty little pond, will, in fact, very likely prove deadly to Grass Parrakeet babies, and a horrible nuisance, to young and old alike, of every species of parrakeet.

Brain or no brain, gnats and mosquitoes *never* go near the big cage which contains the beady eyes of our pet Shama; he just *loves* them! But the wretched things get into the nests of the poor little Grass Parrakeets, biting the babies and terrifying the mothers.

The trouble is that many of these insects bite perhaps a fox, a squirrel or a none-too-healthy stray cat, pick up some nasty infection and then go and pump it into the nearest babies who are unable to get out of their box.

The answer is spray and spray again. Anti-mite is excellent, sprayed on the top, sides and bottom of nest boxes in damp humid weather in the summer.

If there is a pond in the garden, keep the type of fish in it which devour gnats, etc. If there is a compost heap, and if you *must* have one (we do not, although we are keen gardeners) site it as far away as possible from the most vulnerable of all the parrot-type birds dealt with in this book, the Grass Parrakeets.

Spiders
It is an excellent idea to encourage all non-poisonous spiders to live in aviary flights and houses. The birds do not touch them and they catch a lot of winged insects.

Red mites
These are the bane of all canary breeders and bird keepers in general. Red mites look grey until they have fed and filled themselves with some unfortunate bird's blood, when they appear bright red. They come out at night to feed, and skulk in crevices during the day. Good hygiene is the only way to deal with them. Spray Banmite, before and during breeding, round the outside of the boxes and, particularly, on the *ends* of the perches, which is where mites often hide. Also spray any odd crevices in the aviary. Use Antimite during the breeding period.

Birds attacked by red mites will certainly suffer from anaemia, and can also contract a nasty disease called lankesterella. It used to be called atoxoplasma. Birds bitten by red mites will sometimes pull out their feathers because of the irritation.

3
Neophemas   Grass Parrakeets

That colourful and fascinating group of birds, the Australian Grass Parrakeets, are very rightly some of the world's most popular avicultural subjects. In every corner of the globe, where birds are kept and bred, one is likely to find some members of this family.

It would be fairly safe to assume that after budgerigars, cockatiels and lovebirds, more Grass Parrakeets are kept and bred in the UK than any other species of parrot-type bird, and this pattern is likely to be repeated in most parts of the world where aviculture flourishes.

The reasons for this popularity are not difficult to find. Grass Parrakeets' needs are simple; most are hardy, provided they are given a good house; they only need small flights, and they are mostly very willing breeders. All Grass Parrakeets are extremely colourful, and their tiny songs and soft whistles could not possibly offend even the most sensitive ears, which puts them among the number-one choices for those interested in keeping birds, who live in urban areas, or who have close neighbours.

Of all the species of birds we have kept and bred, perhaps the most totally adorable babies were the Bourkes, with their huge dark eyes and incredibly soft plumage. Perhaps it is as well to give a word of warning here: all Grass Parrakeet babies, if handled, are as difficult to hold and 'contain' as mice! They are out of one's hands and 'bang' into the nearest wall, wire or whatever, in a split second, long before they have the faintest chance of being able to fly.

With *all* Grass Parrakeets it is very necessary to put some form of soft netting (garden netting, as used for the protection of fruit bushes would be suitable) at each end of the aviary flight when baby birds are expected out of the nest. This prevents a smashed wing or concussed head.

One other thing is also very important. Make sure that only very shallow water containers are in the aviary when there are young around, and *never* take a deep can of water into an aviary of very young Grass Parrakeets; they have been known to catapult themselves into this strange and interesting object with such force that they were concussed and drowned almost instantly. Concussion is one of the greatest risks to young Grass Parrakeets. So extra care and slow careful movements are best at breeding time.

The diet for all Grass Parrakeets is roughly the same. Being largely seed-eating birds, it is easy to give them a diet which will keep them both healthy and happy. This does not mean to say they do not want and need a reasonable variety of foods. We have always thought of the Turquoisines as our 'poison tasters'; if they eat an unusual wild food, it is safe for other birds in our collection. If they refuse to touch something, then we would suspect it might be poisonous or injurious to all birds.

The basic diet given to our Grass Parrakeets all year round is 35 per cent canary seed, 45 per cent mixed millets, and 20 per cent small mixed sunflower seeds. To this basic mixture various other seeds are added, depending on the time of year, the temperature, and whether or not the birds are breeding. One of the problems with all these little birds is that the cock *will* take all the fatty-oily hemp seeds which are intended for both him *and* his hen. The result is often a cock suffering from fatty kidney-liver syndrome after about three or four years. To try to avoid this problem with a favourite seed which is very good for the birds in cold weather, we throw a small quantity onto the ground, over the seed tray, etc., to give the hen a chance to get her share. We feed between one and two level teaspoonfuls for two birds, the larger quantity being given in colder weather.

Niger seed is richer still in fats and oils, and also in protein, so it is not given at all during the winter months, but reserved for just before the hens start to lay, when each bird is allowed as much as can be held between the first finger and the thumb, or a pinch, as it is known. This means two pinches for two breeding birds. After the third egg is laid, niger is discontinued, because it is contained in many rearing foods, such as Cédé or Nectarblend.

Throughout the winter months we give the birds one teaspoonful per two birds of black rapeseed and linseed, in the proportion of 70 per cent rapeseed to 30 per cent linseed. Both are oil-fat rich.

Some breeders, living in areas where the winter is long and very cold, feed their birds with up to 30 per cent of the above oil-fat and protein-rich seeds. What is not known is how long birds live which are fed in this way. For those breeders who hope their birds will live and thrive for a number of years, it would probably be best to keep the oil-rich seeds to a much lower level, 10 per cent for example, except during exceptionally cold weather.

All our Grass Parrakeets, in fact, all our parrot-type birds, receive brown bread and milk, squeezed out and crumbled, fresh, every day of the year, and twice a day if it is very cold (it freezes hard very quickly), or if it is very hot (when it 'bakes' rock hard). In very hot weather the milk is not included, as even if it is boiled it still seems unpleasant. Then the bread is just made moist with water, and squeezed and crumbled.

During the three winter months, any good powder tonic can be added to the above food. Use one containing the B complex of vitamins, plenty of Vitamins A and D3, and preferably containing the essential amino acids methionine and lysine. When the birds are breeding, a good quality egg-rearing food is added to the bread and milk. The ones we use are either Nectarblend or Cédé rearing food, mixed with Cédé tonic for parrot-type birds, in the proportions, 70 per cent rearing food to 30 per cent tonic food. Cédé foods can be bought from seed merchants or from bird establishments catering for the needs of bird keepers. Many other excellent commercial rearing foods are available.

We have never known a Grass Parrakeet who did not enjoy sweet apple. They eat it through the winter and also devour it to feed to their young. No other fruit seems to interest them, but they are fond of pollen, which is vey good for them as it contains just about every known vitamin, amino acids (the chief part of protein) and many necessary minerals. In the UK, one of the best ways to give birds pollen is to give them hazel (*Corylus*) catkins in the spring, and forget-me-not (*Myosotis*) and wild honeysuckle (*Lonicera periclymenum*) flowers in the summer. These birds are also extremely fond of the seeding heads of the garden forget-me-not.

The popular wild food, chickweed (*Stellaria media*) is not given to our birds, one good reason being that the hens get so fond of it that they furiously attack the poor cocks if the source dries up and there is no more to give them. Also, they tend, for the above reason, to feed far too much of it to the babies, instead of giving them really nourishing rearing foods, so, instead of nice plump babies coming out of the nest, a number of skinny little ones will emerge!

So many public areas, market gardens and farmers' fields are now sprayed with chemicals that it is necessary to be extremely careful about collecting wild food for one's birds. However, if the owner knows of a place where chemicals are not used, or can grow such plants in the garden, the birds will greatly appreciate the seeding heads of shepherd's purse (*Capsella bursa-pastoris*), plaintain (*Plantago major*) and dandelion (*Tarazacum vulgaria*). These will be particularly welcome during breeding.

Grass Parrakeets spend quite a lot of time on the ground, and are therefore the type of birds who need greenfoods, so ours are given some kind of greenfood all year round. Lettuce, green celery tops, cress, endive (a great favourite), chicory, seeding heads of spinach in summer, and small fine grasses and their seeding heads are all enjoyed. Pieces of carrot and celery are speared onto nails driven into the framework of the aviary. During the winter spray millet is given in cold weather to cheer the birds when they are cold, and also well-washed branches from hazel and apple trees. The birds enjoy the buds on the bare branches very much. Any leaves should always be removed before giving the branches.

Like all the other birds dealt with in this book, Grass Parrakeets must be given a constant supply of fresh, clean, mixed, or mineralised, grits, fine oystershell grit, and, most important, fresh, clean cuttlefishbone, secured very firmly. We make holes in the hard shell and 'spear' it onto two nails driven half-way into any convenient wooden part of the aviary. It should be put in a dry place, as the birds will not eat very wet cuttlefishbone. It must be emphasised that the hens need the calcium from cuttlefishbone, which they convert within their bodies (with the aid of Vitamin D3) into a form of calcium which they use to make the eggshells. Baby birds need a supply of cuttlefishbone from their parents to give them the calcium they need to form strong bones.

An adult parrakeet should be wormed with ½ ml of diluted Panacur; one of two and a half months old needs ¼ ml (see Worming, p. 19).

Neophema chrysostoma   The Blue Winged Grass Parrakeet

Of all the Grass Parrakeets normally available to aviculturists, the Blue Winged is by far the most scarce. It seems as though this extremely charming little bird has been completely overshadowed by its more flamboyantly coloured relatives.

This is a great pity because, like all Grass Parrakeets, it has everything to recommend it to those who live in urban areas and do not have large gardens in which to house big aviaries. They are rather hardy birds, gentle and quiet in behaviour and with very soft call notes, but intolerant of very hot dry conditions.

In the wild these birds mainly inhabit wooded areas or sanddunes in coastal areas of Victoria, New South Wales and the eastern parts of South Australia. They also inhabit Tasmania, and can be found here in forest clearings and even orchards. Apparently, they can be seen, even during the breeding season, in flocks of up to 20 birds. This would suggest that such gregarious birds could perhaps be tried, at some future date, on the colony system of breeding.

The Blue Winged Grass Parrakeet is almost identical in size, weight and colouring to the Elegant, except that the dark blue on its wings is much more extensive. There is a band of deep blue on the forehead. The underparts are yellowish, but perhaps a rather duller hue than that of the Elegant. The female is duller in colour than the male, and the most reliable guide to the sex of these birds is given by Professor S.R. Hodges, who bred them for many years. He says that the primary wing feathers of the male are jet black and in the female they are brownish-black. The Professor says that they proved to be the hardiest of the *Neophemas*.

Their needs are the same as for other Grass Parrakeets.

Neophema bourkii   Bourke's Parrakeet

The Bourke is so different from the other Grass Parrakeets kept and bred by aviculturists throughout the world, that it seems almost as though it should belong to another race of birds. The beautiful soft browns, pinks and sky blues of the normal Bourke have made it a most deservedly popular aviary bird, and when this is added to its willingness to breed, its willingness to foster other small birds, and its lovable and affectionate nature, plus its soft and rather mellow warbling calls, it all adds up to one of the first choices for those with limited space, and living in closely built areas where neighbours must be considered.

If there is any small criticism of this wholly attractive bird, it would be to say that it is partly nocturnal. In a mixed collection of various parrot-type birds, this can be disruptive. This is especially true in the summer, when, as parent birds are endeavouring to get their often rebellious young to go to bed, the Bourkes, having slept like sleepy little owls all day (and looking like them too) wake up and call at the tops of their very small soft voices!

Wild Bourkes are distributed over vast arid areas of Australia from Western Australia, through inland areas of southern and central Australia and the north western parts of New South Wales. It has even been found in the southern half of the Northern Territory. The normal Bourke is a bird of about 20 cm (8 in) in length and weighs about 50 g (2 oz), but domesticated ones can be larger. There is usually a pronounced sky-blue band across the forehead, round the eyes and the cheeks is rather greyish-white, the throat and lower part of the cheeks are a pale salmon pink, the head and neck are brown with a pink tinge. The back of the neck, the back and most of the wings are brown with some buff edging. The sides of the wing are bright blue and the upper tail feathers are dark brown. The under tail feathers are pale blue. The primary wing feathers are a beautiful deep violet blue, and the breast is pink and brown, or rosy pink in exceptionally fine males. The eyes are dark brown and large. The female's colours are the same, but her face tends to be whiter and she is usually of a rather duller colour. The young are like the female, and there is less sky blue on the forehead. The wing strips tend to be faint or absent in young males but frequent in females.

Their food, breeding requirements and nestboxes are the same as for other Grass Parrakeets. The number of eggs laid is usually four to five, and the young hatch at 18–19 days, they leave the nest at about four weeks of age. Netting of some kind should be part of each end of the flight to ensure that the young do not dash themselves to pieces when they first come out of the nest. The hen should be rung before breeding commences, so that she is not later mistaken for one of her young.

Bourkes are strong fliers, and, although they will do quite well in a small flight, 1.8 m × 91 cm × 1.8 m high (6 × 3 × 6 ft), they will certainly make very good use of a larger one during their morning and evening activity. The remain rather quiet for much of the rest of the day. Although growing plants or shrubs in their aviaries is not recommended, they are less likely to harm them than any of the other parrakeets dealt with in this book.

They are good tempered birds, and could be kept with cockatiels, provided their nestbox has a much smaller entrance hole than those for the cockatiels (3.75 cm/1½ in should be all right for them); but far better breeding results will be obtained if they are kept on their own, one pair to an aviary.

There are several attractive mutations of Bourkes. The yellow is a soft yellow buff on the back of the wings and upper tail feathers, with the head, neck and breast a soft rosy pink. In the Isabel there is more rosy pink, extending down the back. The colours of the Fallow are mututed browns, with a rather soft dull pink breast. The mutation which has perhaps more admirers than any other member of the Grass Parrakeets, is the Rosa Bourke, at its best an extremely beautiful bird, with the hen being almost as beautifully coloured as the cock. The face carries a lot of white in the female, but in the male almost the whole body, including much of the wings, is a deep rich rosy pink, with brown markings on the edge of the wings, a little patch of blue on the shoulders, and the sides of the rump and under tail feathers pale blue. The upper tail feathers are brown.

Breeders of mutation Bourkes say that the most beautiful colour of all is obtained by breeding a Fallow with a Rosa; this is said to increase the depth of colour.

Neophema elegans The Elegant Grass Parrakeet

Although less brilliantly coloured than its relatives the Turquoisines and Splendids, the Elegant, so aptly named, has a quiet beauty all its own. To see a number of them flying up and down a large aviary in the late summer sunshine is an unforgettable sight, the blue of their wings so admirably shown off by their softly coloured olive gold plumage.

They are slightly longer than the other popular Grass Parrakeets, at about 23 cm (9 in) and their weight is about 50 g (2 oz). Possibly it is the extra length which gives them their truly 'elegant' appearance.

Their distribution in the wild appears to be mainly Western and south western Australia, but they are also found in South Australia, and on the plains of western Victoria.

The normal male has head, neck, back and much of the wings olive green, the upper tail feathers are light grey blue and round the beak there is deep yellow, with paler yellow on the cheeks. The breast is olive yellow and the underparts are bright yellow, sometimes with an orange patch between the legs. The band across the forehead is deep blue, with a sky blue band behind the deep blue. The shoulders and outer parts of the wing are deep blue with an inner band of lighter blue. The primary wing feathers are a deep violet blue. The under tail feathers are yellow. The eye is dark brown. There is no wing stripe.

The female is duller in colour. She occasionally has a slight wing stripe, but she does not have the orange patch on her underparts. The young birds lack the band of blue on the forehead, which appears during the first four to five months of age. Like all the other Grass Parrakeets, their call notes are subdued and very unlikely to cause any difficulties with neighbours.

Our personal experience of Elegants leads us to think that they are not as hardy as the Turquoisines, but would thrive in conditions suitable for Splendids. Their food and other requirements are exactly the same as for the other Grass Parrakeets, including, of course, a plentiful supply of greenfood. The clutch is usually about four to five eggs. The young hatch at about 18 days, and leave the nest at about four weeks of age. Domesticated birds make charming aviary occupants, flying to greet their owners, and some will even come and eat from the hand.

The Elegant now has some extremely beautiful mutations, which, unfortunately, are very scarce in the UK. Perhaps the most strikingly beautiful is the Lutino (yellow) Elegant, where the blue of the normal is replaced by white; otherwise the whole bird is yellow, the cock has scarlet underparts, and the eyes are red. There is also a Cinnamon, a lovely bird with golden tones to its colouring, and a Pied, which has uneven markings of olive green and clear yellow.

Neophema splendida The Splendid Grass Parrakeet (Scarlet Chested Parrakeet)

Out of all of this most captivating and exquisitely coloured genus of small parrakeets, the Splendid invariably evokes the greatest admiration from newcomers to bird keeping, and from those who do not themselves keep birds. We never fail to get a thrill of pleasure when an elderly and truly magnificent cock Splendid draws himself up to his full height with all the majesty of his nine years of age, and turns his glowing crimson scarlet breast squarely towards his admirers on the other side of the wire.

This beautiful bird is only about 20 cm (8 in) in length. An adult bird can weigh up to 50 g (2 oz) but approximately 38 g (1½ oz) is more usual. The outstanding feature of the cock Splendid is his deep satin-like ultramarine blue head. The deep scarlet chest extends, in good specimens, well down the breast and ends in a clearcut line, almost as though drawn with a paint brush. Below this line, his colours are deep yellow, extending down to the undersides of his tail. The back is deep rich green, the wings are dark blue with a broad elongated patch of sky blue, which is very visible at all times. The upper tail feathers are deep green. Young Splendid cocks develop their scarlet breasts slowly over several months.

The hen Splendid, although not so brilliantly coloured as the male, is very attractive and, like her husband, a real character. Her back is deep green, and her breast is of medium green. The blue on her head is slight compared with the male. She has the sky blue on the wings, but not the scarlet chest. Her underparts and under tail feathers are yellow. The young are exactly like her.

Before breeding commences, it really is *very* important to put a ring on the hen if she does not already have one, otherwise, within days of the young coming out of the nest, the unfortunate owner will not have any idea which is the mother and which are the young. Also, another word of warning, *never* put young Splendids and young Turquoisines together unless they are all carefully rung with coloured and numbered rings. They all look alike! Turquoisines are supposed to have a slightly 'bare' eye. In recent years this has become less and less obvious, and, in many cases, has disappeared altogether. Splendids never have the 'bare' look about the eye.

In the wild Splendids are to be found in dry, almost desert-like areas where there is sparse growth of shrubs, or in rather open eucalyptus woodland. These birds inhabit the south eastern parts of Western Australia, through southern Australia, parts of Victoria, New South Wales and as far as the southern western part of Queensland, always in the interior of the country.

On the continent of Europe especially, the rare and beautiful mutations of these immensely and deservedly popular little birds are bred in far greater numbers than in the UK. The only exception is the Blue mutation, which is now being bred so regularly and generally that, although it is much more expensive than the original, or normal as it is known, its charm and appealing colours will no doubt inspire many people with the desire to own and breed specimens of this mutation.

The Blue Splendid cock has the same incredibly shining deep blue head. A blue green back and upper tail feathers admirably show off his delicate peach pink breast and almost white underparts and under tail feathers. In the Blue Splendid, the sky blue on the wings seems to show even more than in his normal counterpart. One of the most beautiful sights is to see Blue Splendid cocks zooming up and down their aviaries in brilliant sunlight, like giant tropical butterflies. The hen Blue Splendid is also a beautiful bird, much more colourful than her normal ancestor. The best specimens have a good medium blue on the breast, green blue on the back and upper tail feathers, a deeper shade of medium blue on the head and cheeks, and soft creamy white underparts and undertail feathers. The long deep sky blue patch on the wings of a Blue Splendid hen make her quite a beauty.

In order to preserve the strength of mutations during the early years, it is the usual practice to put a Blue with a split blue. It does not matter which way round it is, cock or hen, they will produce approximately 50 per cent Blues, cocks and hens, and 50 per cent split blues (normal in appearance) cocks and hens. The normal birds split for any mutation, both cocks and hens, look exactly like the true normals, so it is necessary to acquire stock from a very reliable source, which means an owner who keeps *very careful* records, and, preferably, rings all the birds bred.

In the future there are likely to be very many mutations of Splendids. In the UK White Breasted Blue Splendids are rare and extremely expensive. The cocks are incredibly beautiful, the white front seeming to enhance and add depth to the deep blue on the head and the sky blue on the wings, and the hens, too, are extremely beautiful birds.

Other mutations being bred in Europe are Pied Splendids, Cinnamon, Red Breasted (the yellow underparts are replaced by red), Sea Green, Pastel Blue, Isabel, Sky Blue (similar to the White Breasted, but a more delicate shade of blue), Fallow, Silver, the White Breasted Blue mentioned above, and some rather exotic colour combinations of Sea Green with Isabel, and Pastel Blue Cinnamon. No doubt further mutations will follow; but many of them will need years of careful breeding before they are anything but rather delicate rarities.

Normal Splendids breed willingly, so much so that to avoid problems with egg binding and eggs failing to hatch because of chilling in cold weather, nestboxes should always be removed in the autumn and should not be put up again until the temperature is a fairly reliable 15° C (60° F).

A suitable nestbox size is 17.5 × 17.5 cm (7 × 7 in) internal measurement, by 30 cm (12 in) deep, with an entrance hole 3.5 cm (1½ in) in diameter. As with all birds, there should be a perch outside and inside the entrance hole, and a ladder inside the box. The nesting material should be put in the box dry; brown peat mixed with a little compacted pet litter is suitable for these birds. Like Turquoisines, the hens usually scratch and scrape away at the nesting material until they have nearly, or quite, reached the bare bottom of the box. We always make a mound of the nest material at the back of the box, leaving one front corner, with a little hole, with very little nest material at the bottom. This saves the hen's energies for the all-important egg laying.

Most, but not all, hen Splendids will tolerate inspection of the nest while they are laying eggs. Some really want the attention and come dashing out of the nest if one does not go and admire their handiwork, as though they were saying, 'Hey, see what I have done!' All of them want their baby birds admired! The usual clutch of eggs for normals is about five, but Blues tend to lay about three to four eggs. Most, but not all, Splendids are double-brooded, and many normals will try to go to nest a third time. This should be avoided, as it is far too great a strain on the parent birds. Blue Splendids are sometimes only single-brooded.

The eggs take about 19–20 days to hatch. At this time some hens resent being disturbed, but a few days after the first one or two chicks have hatched, the hen will want the admiration and attention of her owner! In the early days, the cock feeds the hen, and the hen feeds the young, so that the food is double-digested. Later, after about ten days, when the hen stops brooding the young in the daytime, he may be allowed into the box to help with the feeding.

It is at this time of year that seeding heads of dandelion, those of very small grasses, and of the garden (forget-me-not) are appreciated. I do not feed chickweed at any time; it can harbour the eggs of internal worms harmful to birds, such as roundworms and hairworms. The seeding heads of shepherd's purse are greatly appreciated, as those of the sow thistle. Pieces of fresh sweet apple are very important to Splendids, and should be given daily. Carrot and celery pieces can be speared onto nails in the wooden uprights close to a perch. The last two can be given about twice a week on alternative days. Splendids are big eaters, so a careful watch must be kept during breeding; they eat surprisingly large quantities of food. Their dietary needs and food requirements during breeding are the same as other Grass Parrakeets and are dealt with fully on page 26.

Neophema pulchella   The Turquoisine

The glittering beauty and magnetic charm of the Turquoisine Grass Parrakeet has probably gained it more admirers than any other member of the *Neophema* genus, with possible exception of the Splendid. In character they could hardly be more different. The Splendid is a little 'bulldog', slow to quarrel, but stubborn, and extremely affectionate towards its owners. The Turquoisines also show great affection towards those who keep and breed them, but their temperament is extremely volatile, they are quick to pick a quarrel, extremely active, and we have found them to be much hardier and tougher than Splendids.

In the wild the areas of Australia which they inhabit are much more limited than those of the Splendids: the south eastern parts of Queensland, as far as the coast, New South Wales and parts of Victoria where there are woodlands, open forest land and rivers and streams. They also frequent the national parks in the eastern part of New South Wales.

It is interesting to note, however, that there do not seem to be any recorded instances of long life, as with Splendids. We know of one hen Splendid (not ours) who was successfully fostering young birds at the age of 12, and a male Splendid who was actually fathering young at that age. One of our own pairs of normal Splendids is still breeding happily at nine years of age. Our Turquoisines have not so far exceeded six or seven years of age. They certainly seem to be rather prone to fatty kidney-liver syndrome after about four or five years of age, no doubt due to their fondness of oil-rich seeds. In recent years we have adopted a policy of extreme care with the distribution of oil-rich seeds, even in the cold winter months, in an effort to prevent this trying and often fatal condition.

Much lower temperatures can be tolerated by Turquoisines than would be wise for Splendids, especially young ones during their first year. Of course, Turquoisines, and all *Neophemas*, must be provided with a good house which can be completely closed in the winter months. Although we live in the southern half of the UK, it is very cold; the temperature can drop to −10° C (14° F) or even lower each winter, so we always totally enclose all the *Neophema* aviaries in PVC sheeting.

We think light is of much more importance than heat, so nearly all our enclosures have an electric light, which is turned high for the first three hours of darkness, then very low for the night. This way the birds can see to eat, and regain their perches if they suffer a night fright.

Turquoisines are ideal birds for those living in urban areas. Just like Splendids, their little songs and calls could not possibly disturb anyone. Perhaps their only drawback, if it can be considered one, is that when a number of young ones are kept together through the winter, for ease of management, they do tend to quarrel, but usually all is peace and quiet again after a few minutes.

The normal Turquoisine is a bird of many contrasting colours, making it one of nature's beauties. Its length is 20 cm (8 in), and its weight about 50 g (2 oz). The cock's head and face are a glittering iridescent shade of mid-blue, much lighter in colour than that of the Splendid. The back is brilliant deep green, and the breast is a deep rich yellow and this extends right through to the under side of the tail. The upper side of the tail is bright dark green, as are part of the wings, but one of the features of all male Turquoisines (and some older females) is the elongated band of rich crimson on the wings. The primary wing feathers are a beautiful shade of violent blue.

The hen has much quieter colours, but is nearly always a tremendous character, ordering her life, and very often that of her partner, with mock screams issuing from her tiny wide-open mouth, with all the force of a little sergeant major. Male Turquoisines quickly learn to respect their partners' wishes! Her head is the same blue but with only an indication on the brow and cheeks. Her breast is light greenish-yellow, her wings are green and blue like the male, the under side of the tail is greenish yellow, the upper side and the back are bright dark green. A few hens do have the crimson patch on the wings; and many young males come out of the nest with this marking, which is very useful for identification. There are under wing stripes on both sexes and we have not found this a reliable guide to the sexing of young birds. Rather a better guide is the presence of the crimson band at an early age, and a generally more brilliant look about the head. The young are exactly like the mother, hence the importance of ringing the mother before breeding commences.

Years ago it was easy to tell young Splendids from young Turquoisines, as all the Turquoisines had bare 'eye rings' – not any longer. Quite often hens possess this feature, but not the cocks.

Baby Turquoisines are even more likely to dash themselves to pieces than Splendids, so great care is necessary, and *shallow-water trays only*. Young Turquoisines can, if they really must, feed themselves at five days out of the nest. But it is only the occasional cock who will attack the young, and then mainly the young cocks. Most are tolerant and excellent parents, feeding their young and cleaning their beaks afterwards with tremendous care and delicacy. The brooding time is the same as for Splendids; they usually lay about five eggs, and the young will emerge at about four weeks of age. Turquoisines need exactly the same nestboxes and nesting material as Splendids.

The diet and feeding at breeding time are the same as for all Grass Parrakeets and are given on page 26.

Like the Splendid, the turquoisine has mutated into some startlingly beautiful colours, but there is a difference. Some of the most brilliantly coloured Turquoisines are not considered to be mutations, because they are arrived at by selective breeding. The lovely Orange and Red and Scarlet Bellied ones are an example. These wonderful 'sunset' colours are now a feature of many Turquoisines, the hen having an orange red or deep red patch between her legs, extending almost to her breast in some cases, while the cock's fiery colours often extend well up towards, or into, his breast. These birds now breed only birds similar to themselves; there do not appear to be any reversions to the wild, normal colour amongst them.

Another much rarer colour arrived at by selective breeding is the Red Fronted Turquoisine. Thus is the patience of the breeders well rewarded! The Red Fronted cock develops his wonderful crimson scarlet breast and underparts slowly, in the same manner as the Splendid cock. His wing patch is large and bright crimson scarlet, and the rest of his body is as for the normal. The hen has a brilliant crimson scarlet belly, extending well up towards the breast, which is the colour of the normal hen.

The mutations of the Turquoisines are as many and varied as those of the Splendid. The Yellow mutation (it is known as *Yellow*, not Lutino) with its pale sky blue head, shoulders, brilliant scarlet wing patch, and glowing scarlet belly, extending up towards the breast, has to be seen to be believed; its beauty is breathtaking. To Freddie and me it is the most beautiful of all small parrakeets.

These yellow mutations seem to have even more character than their normal forbears, if it is possible to say that of such a lively and charming race of birds. Certainly they tend to be extremely friendly towards their owners, invariably greeting them by zooming about their aviaries like butterflies or, in the case of the hens, sometimes sitting absolutely still with their great dark eyes shining out of a golden yellow face. The hen usually has the beautiful scarlet belly, and also very pale blue shoulders, but she has only a very little blue on her head.

When breeding from Yellows, it is advisable to put a Yellow cock or hen (it does not matter which) with a split yellow partner. That way the strength of the race is preserved, the size is preserved, and the owner has not had to make such a large outlay of money for a pair of birds. All small birds can sometimes depart this life with surprising speed, and not through any mismanagement on the part of the unfortunate owner. This applies to all small species; if things go wrong, it is not always possible to save them. Things usually happen more slowly with large birds, and, in any case, it is much easier to care for them if they are ill.

The other mutations so far produced, and mainly to be found on the continent of Europe are: the Fallow, the most common after the Yellow, but not nearly so beautifully coloured; the Pied – these are a mixture of greens, yellow and blues, and rather variable in colouring; the very rare Pastel Blues, and the Olives. Some breeders, in the UK and in other parts of Europe, are succeeding in producing a Red Fronted Yellow – beauty beyond nature's wildest dreams!

4
Polytelis   Parrakeets

There are three members of this genus. All are extremely popular as aviary birds throughout the world, and with very good reasons. Their colours are beautiful, and they are all friendly and often fearless by nature. On the whole they breed reasonably freely. In the UK they cannot be classed as expensive birds to buy, but, on the other hand, they do maintain their value, so the breeder who has young to sell does get some return for the original cost of buying, and, because they are so popular, there should never be any problem in selling young birds.

To avoid difficulties with neighbours, it must be pointed out that these birds can make a fair amount of noise, especially Princess of Wales Parrakeets. During the breeding season the cocks call incessantly, and we do mean incessantly! This can lead to complaints from neighbours; the cock's voice is extremely penetrating and can be heard up to 201 m (220 yd) away.

Barrabands' voices, which appear louder close by, do not 'carry' nearly so far, but they are clever imitators. A cock we had at one time used to imitate the wild owls so well that they called back to him! A Rock Peplar pair we had were most lovable, friendly birds, steady and quiet, but, most unfortunately, the hen died. We then got another partner for the male because he seemed so lonely. She had a call exactly like a goose, and, as we have close neighbours, we really could not risk being accused of keeping geese in an urban area! They had to go, and promptly presented their new owner with a nestful of delightful young! All *Polytelis* need large flights. The Princess of Wales, that most elegant of birds, is especially active. The hens tend to be slightly dominant, so, in practice, there is very little bullying, which means that a large house is not necessary. Of course, they do need a comfortable place where they can be shut in during extremely cold weather.

Feeding *Polytelis* Parrakeets does not present any problems. They will thrive on a diet of sunflower seeds, oats, wheat, canary seed, mixed millets, spray millet, pine nuts, a little hemp seed in cold weather, and any shelled nuts the owner cares to offer. These parrakeets are fond of peanuts, but the owner is warned to take note of the fact that many peanuts offered for sale to bird keepers are really not fit to be given to one's birds; they can also be infected with the aflatoxin mould, so take care and watch the health of the birds.

Our Barrabands, Princess of Wales and Rock Peplars always had a supply of brown bread and milk, squeezed out and crumbled, fresh daily, all the year round, and given twice daily at breeding time and as bread and water in hot weather. When the birds are breeding, a good egg-rearing mixture should be added to the bread and milk. Fruit is very much enjoyed by all these birds – apple, pear or orange, cut in half, well sugared, and speared on two headless nails on a flat surface was a tremendous favourite with the Barrabands and Rock Peplars. Pomegranite, cut up into pieces they can hold in their claws, is greatly enjoyed by all the larger parrakeets. In fact it is one of the greatest treats one can give them. Pieces of celery and carrot speared on nails are also enjoyed.

All these birds enjoy branches, minus their leaves, but with the buds left on; the best ones to give are all kinds of willow (*salix*), apple, and hazel (*Corylus*). They are all extremely fond of berries, such as those of mountain ash, otherwise known as rowan (*Sorbus aucuparia*), the common hawthorn (*Crataegus monogyna*) and, of course, the common elder (*Sambucus nigra*). All will be devoured immediately they are put in the flights.

The usual greenfoods mentioned for other birds in this book are all enjoyed: lettuce, endive, sprouted cress and mustard, seeding spinach and chicory will all be eaten. Seeding grasses, seeding head of dandelion (*Taraxacum vulgaria*), sow thistle (*Sorchus oleraceus*), knapweed (*Centaurea nigra*) and shepherd's purse (*Capsella bursa pastoris*) will all be greatly appreciated, as will the flowers of the wild honeysuckle (*Lonicera periclymenum*).

If, as is so often the case, it is necessary to roof the flights to protect the birds from predators, they will greatly appreciate a gentle spray of water in fine weather. They will always try to get into gentle summer rain to bathe. All of them enjoy scratching around on the floor of their flights so, as with all other parrot-type birds, they must be given worming medicine at least twice a year. It should be noted that Princess of Wales Parrakeets are extremely easily stressed, so plenty of whistles, or words of encouragement and reassurance, should be given to them while they are being wormed.

Polytelis swainsonii The Barraband

This elegant and handsome representative of the *Polytelis* genus is very justly popular both with experienced aviculturists and newcomers to bird keeping. For those who can afford the space for a fairly large aviary, and who either do not have neighbours, or have tolerant ones, the Barraband is an excellent choice; it is, in any case, not nearly as noisy as a Princess of Wales Parrakeet.

The distribution of these birds in their native Australia is limited to inland New South Wales and the northern parts of Victoria, where they inhabit woodlands and riversides.

One great advantage of these attractice birds is that, when adult, the male and female are so extremely easy to tell apart. The general colour of the male above and below is a bright, rich green, including most of the wings and upper tail feathers. The outer parts of the primary wing feathers are dull blue, the under tail feathers are black. The back of the head has a slight bluish 'wash', the whole of the crown, forehead and cheeks is a bright rich yellow, and at the lower edge of the yellow cheeks there is a bright scarlet crescent or 'necklace'; in good specimens this can be very wide and prominent. The beak is a handsome coral pink and the eye is orange. The length of a Barraband is about 40 cm (16 in) and the weight of a male is about 154 g (6 oz); the female may weigh a little more.

The hen is attractively, but differently, coloured. She has a slightly duller green colour, and does not have the yellow on the face and head, or the red band round the front of the neck. Instead she has a faintly pinkish tinge on the front of her neck. Her thighs are yellow orange or sometimes scarlet. The upper tail feathers are green, the under tail feathers are deep pink near the vent and the rest are dull brownish-green margined with pink. The eyes are yellow. The young birds look exactly like the hen, except that the young cocks may be a brighter green, and may show a faint outline of the yellow and red, which will develop slowly over a period of about 18 months. Both sexes have the pink marginal tail feathers at first. The young males are more likely to call and warble than the females.

Before actual breeding takes place, the hen has to establish that her partner can and will feed her and her young. So she 'begs' incessantly (and noisily) for food, with a bobbing action of her head. This pattern is not special to Barrabands; many of the larger Australian parrakeets behave in a similar fashion. It should be emphasised that this begging noise is quite low pitched and does not carry far.

Usually about five eggs are laid, and the young hatch after about 20 days, leaving the nest at about five to six weeks of age.

Barrabands are extremely fond of honey. We gave ours half-oranges sweetened with honey during the winter; unfortunately this was not possible in the summer as too many wasps and bees were attracted to the honey. Another way to give the birds the nectar they obviously desire is to give them flowers, such as wild honeysuckle. They enjoy almost any fruit, and are extremely fond of berries of every kind.

The nestbox and nesting materials can be the same as for Rock Peplars: 91 cm (3 ft) deep by 25 sq cm (10 sq in) with an entrance hole of 8.75 cm (3½ in) in diameter. Dowelling perches 1.6 cm (⅝ in) in diameter, must be fitted below the entrance hole, about 12.5 cm (5 in) below on the outside and 10 cm (4 in) below on the inside of the box. A good ladder inside the box is necessary.

Polytelis alexandrae   The Princess of Wales Parrakeet

Princess of Wales Parrakeets are far and away the most elegant of the three members of the *Polytelis* genus. Their soft colours seem like a permanent reminder of a glorious English spring day; apple blossom pinks, soft light yellow green and those beautiful pale and violet blues. Thoughts of wild violets and apple orchards under a blue sky come flooding into one's mind at the sight of these lovely birds.

The distribution of these birds in their native country is over a large part of Western Australia, the northern parts of South

Australia, and into the southern parts of the Northern Territory.

A very noticeable feature of Princess of Wales Parrakeets is their almost dove-like heads, quite unlike any other parrakeet, while the cock has an unusual spatula-shaped tip to one primary wing feather on each wing.

The male's considerable length is mostly tail; the two central tail feathers bring him up to 45 cm (18 in) in length, with a weight of about 99 g (3½ oz). The hen weighs very slightly more. The cock's head and forehead are bright pale blue, the throat and the front of the neck, running down to the breast, are soft pink, the back and parts of the wings are a soft olive green, the shoulders and a large patch on the wings are bright light green, and the upper parts of the primaries are dull blue. The upper tail feathers are olive green, some feathers being tinged with pink. The tip of the tail is blue and the under tail feathers are dull green. The thighs are rosy pink and the rump is blue, or, in older males, deep purple. The breast is blue grey, or green grey; the eye is orange and the beak is red.

The hen's colours are similar but duller, and she has a shorter tail which sometimes is a more pronounced pink than that of the male, also her beak is often a duller red. The colour of her rump is very much duller, usually a grey blue. The young are similar to the female, except that the young males may have more blue on the crown of the head.

Anyone who has kept these delightful birds will have quickly noticed their fearless, rather more than tame, behaviour. They quickly learn to eat from the hand. Unfortunately, they are 'jumpy' birds, and easily startled, as an experience of ours illustrates. Someone tending them left both doors of the entrance porch to the aviary open one summer morning. Coming round a corner in the garden I was confronted by two little 'bodies' (the pair of Princess of Wales) walking sedately down the path, side by side. All our birds have names, unless they are just bred and must be sold. I was able to call them by name and get them to turn right round and make their way back to their aviary, equally sedately.

Just as they got to the entrance a huge wild wood pigeon flew over very low; they were terrified, and instantly rose up into the air together. I had not dared to put down a pile of (breakable) feed bowls I was carrying in my right hand, so I had an 'enth' of a split second to decide which to catch. The cock was nearest my left hand, which shot up almost automatically, and I caught him by one leg and 'shooed' him back into his aviary. The hen, meanwhile, flew the entire length of the ridge of the hill on which we live, up and down, straight as an arrow, many, many times, a most lovely sight, but hardly one I could enjoy. The cock yelled at the top of his very considerable voice all morning and most of the afternoon. Eventually, the hen got hungry and came down to eat and I was able to guide her into the safety of the entrance porch and then into her aviary. The fact that she had eggs in her nest probably did help to bring her back, coupled with the cock's distress.

Unfortunately, these lovely and wholly attractive birds have one great disadvantage; they are noisy, before and during the breeding season, especially the cock, who calls just non-stop, from dawn till after dusk. He will even 'yell' in the night if something frightens him, bringing the hen off her nest because she wants to see what is happening! We lost five superb, fully feathered baby birds that way one year; it was unusually cold and they all died.

Nestboxes for Princess of Wales are discussed in the chapter on Housing, as is the flight size for these very active birds. There is an alternative to the L-shaped box, so much used by breeders of these birds, to avoid the rather clumsy hens jumping down and smashing their eggs. This idea comes from an American breeder, writing in the American Federation of Aviculture's magazine *The Watchbird* in June-July 1987. Roger Brigas suggests using a 30 × 30 × 30 cm (12 × 12 × 12 in) box with entry hole 7.5 (3 in) in diameter, with the usual dowel perch going between 7.5 cm and 12.5 cm (3 and 5 in) *inside* the box as well as outside. This makes it much more difficult for the hen to dive into the box and down onto the eggs at speed. He gives his birds at least 7.5 cm (3 in) of wood shavings as nesting material.

These birds can be very long lived. Rosemary Low, in *Parrots, Their Care and Breeding*, records one of 23 years of age.

When breeding, these birds should be given the usual brown bread and milk, made crumbly, with a good rearing food, plus some frozen sweet corn, cooked for about one minute and well rinsed or, better still, some fresh corn on the cob. They are also fond of green peas. They enjoy all the usual fruits, berries and greenfoods, and will greatly enjoy branches of apple, willow and hazel in the winter months. A good powder tonic, containing the B complex of vitamins, should be given to them during the winter and spring.

The mutations of the Princess of Wales are extraordinarily beautiful, the Lutino is a deep rich colour, often with pink under the chin and under the tail. A Red mutation has occurred in Australia, and the Blues can be a light blue grey or a darker blue and grey; the Blue mutation is variable. There is also an Albino, and no doubt other colours will follow.

Polytelis anthopeplus   The Rock Peplar

This quietly attractive member of the *Polytelis* genus, although perhaps not as popular as the more showy Barraband, and certainly having many fewer admirers than the beautiful and elegant Princess of Wales, nevertheless is kept by many aviculturists, who often become extremely fond of these birds. They are altogether quieter and more sedate in their movements than either the Barraband or the Princess of Wales – probably hand-reared ones would be delightfully tame. Normally these birds are not noisy, although their call note is perhaps more powerful than that of the Barraband, but, in comparison to the continuous noise made by a Princess of Wales cock in breeding condition, any calls they do make are of short duration, and do not carry far.

The distribution of Rock Peplars in the wild state is confined to two areas, in the eastern one the birds are to be found in woodland areas around the Murray River, in the south west of New South Wales, the northern parts of Victoria and the eastern parts of South Australia. The larger area where these birds are found is in the southern parts of Western Australia.

The male cock Peplar varies considerably in colour; the best ones are nearly yellow, others are a dull olive green. The crown and back of the neck are a bright olive green yellow, the breast and underparts are a bright deep yellow, the back and upper parts of the wings are deep olive green, the primary wing feathers are blue black, and there is a wide band of red across part of the wing. The upper tail feathers are black and dark green, the under tail feathers are black. The beak is coral red and the eye orange brown. The length of the cock is about 40 cm (16 in) and the weight is about 170 g (nearly 6 oz); the hen can be even larger. They are the largest member of the *Polytelis* genus, and many people find them the most willing breeders.

The female is mainly olive green in colour, but the colour can be brighter on the rump, breast and between the legs. The hen's tail feathers are tipped with pink on the under side, her beak is a duller shade of coral, and her eyes are brown.

Young birds are the same in appearance as the female, except that the young males are often a more yellow green on the head and breast. They acquired adult plumage at about 15 months old and are usually ready to breed at about two years of age, although it has been known for them to breed at only 11 months old, according to Rosemary Low, in the revised edition of *Parrots, Their Care and Breeding*. They usually lay about four eggs, which take about 21 days to hatch, and the young leave the nest at around six weeks of age.

All birds should be kept as clean as possible, but especially Rock Peplars. They can be subject to eye complaints, so perches should be regularly cleaned, and, of course, the birds must be wormed regularly twice a year. They do not tolerate damp conditions, and should be provided with a comfortable house into which they can be shut on winter nights. The size of aviary suitable for them and the other members of the *Polytelis* genus is given in the Housing chapter.

The size of nestbox suitable for Rock Peplars is about 91 cm (3 ft) deep by 25 sq cm (10 sq in) (outside measurement) with an entrance hole 9 cm (3½ in) in diameter. A 1.6 cm ($^5/_8$ in) dowelling perch must be fitted to go through, from outside to inside the box, below the entrance hole, and, of course, there must be a ladder inside the box. Nesting material can be rotted wood, compressed pet litter, and some peat.

5

Psephotus Parrakeets

Only two members of this genus of birds can be said to qualify as popular parrakeets in aviculture; the others are either almost extinct, rare and in the possession of a few very experienced aviculturists, or, in the case of the Blue Bonnets (*P. haematogaster*), extremely difficult to breed because they nest early in the year and cease brooding their young at ten days, with the result that the babies frequently die from the effects of chilling in cold weather.

The Paradise Parrakeet (*P. pulcherrimus*) is so rare now as to be considered almost extinct. The Golden Shouldered (*P. chrysopterygius*) is extremely rare, but a few do come into the possession of experienced (and wealthy) aviculturists occasionally.

The Hooded (*P. chrysopterygius dissimilis*) is being bred by a few very experienced aviculturists in the UK and, no doubt, is established in many other countries as well. Its habit of nesting (if it nests at all) in the winter months make it far from easy to manage.

The Redrumped Parrakeet (*P. haematonotus*), in contrast to its relatives, is one of the easiest of all parrakeets to keep, probably the best foster parent of any parrot-type bird, and so easy to obtain, breed and maintain that it is one of the very best birds for a newcomer to bird keeping. The slightly more colourful Many Coloured, or Mulga Parrot as it is also known (*P. varius*), does not have a reputation for ease of management and free breeding like its more popular relative, the Redrump.

Redrumps and Many Coloureds should be given a wide range of seeds, sunflower, canary, millets, oats, with a little black rapeseed and linseed, plus hempseed in the winter, brown bread and milk squeezed out and made crumbly and, when breeding, any good egg-rearing food should be added. They will enjoy apple, corn on the cob, cooked sweet corn and spring millet. Branches of willow (*Salix*), apple and hazel (*Corylus*) will be enjoyed during the winter months. They are fond of greenfood and should be given as wide a variety as possible. Lettuce, endive, chicory, cress, sprouted rapeseed, seeding spinach and pieces of carrot and celery should all be offered to them. Wild foods such as wild honeysuckle (*Lonicera periclymenum*) the seeding heads of knapweed (*Centaurea nigra*), dandelion (*Taraxacum vulgaria*) and sow thistle (*Sonchus oleraceus*) will all be appreciated. Great care must be taken to make sure that any wild foods are not contaminated with insecticide sprays.

Aviaries suitable for Redrumps and Many Coloureds can be found in the chapter on Housing.

These birds need to be wormed at least twice a year with about ¾ ml of Panacur 2.05 solution without additives, diluted as one part of Panacur to five parts of water. As, like many birds, they are resentful of this procedure, it is easiest to give the medicine in the side of the mouth, from a syringe without a tube.

Psephotus varius   Many Coloured Parrakeet (Mulga Parrot)

The Many Coloured Parrakeet, or Mulgar Parrot as it is sometimes known, is a more colourful member of the *Psephotus* genus than the Redrump, but it is not nearly so willing to breed as its more prolific and popular relative.

In the wild the distribution of Many Coloureds is to be found over a huge part of Australia, stretching from Western Australia through the southern parts of Northern Territory, to South Australia, parts of Victoria, New South Wales and into southern Queensland.

The length and weight of the Many Coloured are the same as the Redrump. The male's plumage is mostly a deep green. He has a golden yellow band across his forehead and a little red patch on the back of his head. The face, throat and breast are bright green; the lower parts are a paler green, heavily marked with orange red. There is a bright yellow patch high on the wings and a large patch of violet blue below, merging into the primary wing feathers. The upper tail feathers are dark blue; the under tail feathers are pale blue, tipped with white. The rump is green, the beak is grey, the eyes are brown.

The female has head, back and breast of brown olive, with an orange band across the forehead, and a red patch on the back of her head. The lower parts are pale green, sometimes with some red or orange between the legs. She has a red patch high on the shoulder and on the bend of the wing, and the primary wing feathers are a paler shade of violet blue than the male's. The upper tail feathers are dull olive green tinged with blue; the under tail feathers are pale green. The beak is grey, the eyes are brown. The young are duller in colour than the adults, and attain their full colours at about six months of age. The young males show some red on the underparts before this time.

Many Coloured Parrakeets are apt to try to nest early in the year, so the nestbox, which can be the same as that supplied to their relatives, the Redrumps, should be placed in a very sheltered position in the aviary. Suitable sized aviaries for these birds are to be found in the chapter on Housing.

About four to six eggs form the clutch, and the eggs take about 19-20 days to hatch. The hen stops brooding the young when they are about 14 days old, which can lead to trouble if the birds go to nest early in cold climates. Perhaps one answer would be for a low-wattage light bulb in an enclosed area below the nest box. The young remain in the nest for about 30 days, sometimes a little longer. A careful watch must be kept on the adult male once the young come out of the nest, in case he attacks the young males.

When the birds are breeding, as well as the usual brown bread and milk with an egg-rearing food, the parents will appreciate frozen sweet corn, cooked for one minute and well rinsed.

B.R. Hutchins and R.H. Lovell writing on Mulga Parrots in their book *Australian Parrots, A Field and Aviary Study*, recommend that Many Coloured or Mulga Parrots should not be allowed to breed until they are two years of age. It should also be noted that these birds do not tolerate damp conditions well. At present there do not appear to be any mutations of this very attractive bird, whose call notes and song are soft and pleasant.

Psephotus haematonotus Redrump Parrakeet

This is the bird which starts so many newcomers to bird keeping on their way to one of the world's most enduring and fascinating pastimes. The person who keeps Redrumps one year will very likely be keeping not only Redrumps five, ten or fifteen years later, but a lot of other parrakeets and parrots as well! This is also the bird which is still used by many people to foster rarer species, or neglected young, but, if fostering, it must be remembered that the Redrump young leave the nest at about four weeks old, so any birds which take longer may not be fed after that time.

The distribution of these parrakeets is restricted to the south eastern part of Australia. They are to be found in New South Wales in wooded country, and by riversides in Victoria and in eastern parts of South Australia.

The length of the cock is about 27 cm (10½ in) and his weight is about 65 g (2½ oz). The male's colours are mainly green, bluish-green on the forehead and cheeks, and green on the back of the head. The throat and breast are yellow green, the lower parts are yellow, the shoulders and back are blue green, the bend of the wing and primary wing feathers are violet blue, the rump is red, the upper tail feathers are bright bronzy green with a blue tinge to some of the feathers, the under tail feathers are pale blue white, the beak is black and the eyes are brown. The female has a grey forehead and cheeks with an olive tinge, the breast has a lighter, more yellow tinge to the grey, the back and shoulders are a dull olive green, the rump is bright green and the upper tail feathers are bright deep green. The under tail feathers are nearly white with a pale blue tinge. The bend of the wing and parts of the primary wing feathers are a violet blue, but duller than the cock's. The lower parts are yellow white. The beak is dark grey, the eyes are brown.

The young are the same as the adults, but much duller and the young males have only a little red on the rump. The beaks of young males are grey, and of young females yellow. The young birds usually moult at about four months, and attain their adult plumage at this time.

Usually four to six eggs form the clutch, which takes about 18–19 days to hatch. The young leave the nest at about four weeks of age. A careful watch must be kept on the adult male, as at this time he is likely to attack the young males. If necessary, he might have to be put in an adjoining aviary, leaving the female with the young.

All *Psephotus* Parrakeets are extremely aggressive, and the

Splendid Parrakeets (*Neophema splendida*), normal split Blue cock with Blue hen

Bourke's Parrakeet (*Neophema bourkii*)
normal cock

Rosa Bourke (*Neophema bourkii*)

Yellow Bourke (*Neophema bourkii*)

Isabel Bourke (*Neophema bourkii*)

Splendid normal cock (*Neophema splendida*)

Elegant cock (*Neophema elegans*)

Blue Winged Grass Parrakeet (*Neophema chrysostoma*)

Splendid normal hen (*Neophema splendida*)

Blue Splendid pair (*Neophema splendida*)

Turquoisine normal Orange Bellied pair (*Neophema pulchella*)

Yellow Turquoisine cock (*Neophema pulchella*)

Yellow Turquoisine hen and Red Fronted split Yellow cock (*Neophema pulchella*)

Adelaide Rosella (*Platycercus Adelaidae*)

Mealy Rosella (*Platycercus adscitus palliceps*)

Golden Mantled Rosella pair (*Platycercus eximinius cecilae*)

Yellow Rosella (*Platycercus flaveolus*)

Stanley hen (*Platycercus icterotis*)

Stanley cock (*Platycercus icterotis*)

Barraband cock (*Polytelis swainsonii*)

Pennant (Crimson Rosella) cock (*Platycercus elegans*)

Princess of Wales cock (*Polytelis alexandrae*)

Barraband hen (*Polytelis swainsonii*)

Rock Peplar cock (*Polytelis anthopeplus*)

Red Fronted Kakariki (*Cyanoramphus novaezelandiae*)

Yellow Fronted Kakariki (*Cyanoramphus auriceps*)

Redrump normal pair (*Psephotus haematonotus*)

Yellow Redrump cock (*Psephotus haematonotus*)

Yellow Redrump hen (*Psephotus haematonotus*)

Many Coloured cock (*Psephotus varius*)

Moustached cock (*Psittacula alexandrii fasciata*)

Alexandrine cock (*Psittacula eupatria*)

Plum Headed cock (*Psittacula cyanocephala*)

Plum Headed hen (*Psittacula cyanocephala*)

Indian Ringneck cock (*Psittacula krameri manillensis*)

Grey Indian Ringneck (*Psittacula krameri manillensis*)

Blue Indian Ringneck cock (*Psittacula krameri manillensis*)

Cinnamon Indian Ringneck (*Psittacula krameri manillensis*)

Lutino Indian Ringneck at four months old (*Psittacula krameri manillensis*)

saying 'Put two Redrump cocks in an aviary one night, and the next morning there will be one dead Redrump cock' is very true. This is perhaps the only fault this most attractive little bird has. Its character and the loyalty of the cocks to the hens, and vice versa, make them in all respects, most attractive birds to keep, being of a playful nature and with no loud calls, only a sweet little twittering song.

The nestbox should be 45 cm (18 in) deep by 17.5 cm sq (7 in sq)(internal measurement), with an entrance hole of 7.5 cm (3 in). A perch running through from the outside to inside the box, plus a ladder, should be satisfactory. Peat moss, rotted wood and a little compressed pet litter can be used for nesting material, which should be placed in the box to a depth of about 10 cm (4 in). These birds have very strong characters, as has already been mentioned, and it is advisable, once the nestbox has been chosen, to allow the birds to breed in the same one each year. It can be cleaned out thoroughly, and the entrance hole blocked, at the end of each breeding season.

It is most unwise to house two members of the *Psephotus* genus in adjoining aviaries. Even with double-wire, which would be essential to prevent the cocks injuring each other, it would still lead to a lot of squabbling. Cocks and hens, once pair-bonded, that is to say, having mated and perhaps reared a family, should not be parted; they grow extremely fond of each other. Their feeding and rearing requirements are given under the general notes on page 49–50).

There is a very popular and attractive mutation of the normal Redrump. This is the Yellow Redrump, and probably more of these are bred than normals. Jim Hayward, writing in *Cage and Aviary Birds* about his visit to New South Wales, reports seeing a Cinnamon mutation and three Lutino cocks with red eyes and yellow and cream plumage with a brilliant red rump; the hens are cream and white. He also reported seeing a Pied hen Redrump.

6
Platycercus The Rosellas

The Rosella genus of parrakeets presents to the aviculturist some of Australia's most brilliantly coloured species. In no other bird can be found the contrasting reds, whites, blues, golds, blacks and greens so flamboyantly displayed as in the very justly popular and plentiful Golden Mantled Rosella (*Platycercus eximius*). In contrast is the elegant beauty of the rare Brown's Parrakeet (*Platycercus venustus,*) with its blacks and whites, violet blues and pale creamy yellows.

Between these two birds, the one so universally kept throughout the world and the other in the possession of only a few aviculturists scattered over the globe, there are six more members of this brilliantly plumaged genus of birds. All are beautiful, some are brilliantly coloured, all are hardy birds, some of them, like the Golden Mantled Rosella and the Stanley Rosella, breed freely, and none of them exceptionally noisy. All of them can be relied upon to adorn a garden aviary with grace and colour without making special demands on the time of the owner. The young of some, like the Stanley Rosella, are amusing and fascinating to watch when they play together, and generally make their little characters felt to their parents and owners.

Rosellas are strong, hardy birds, much less likely to suffer from frostbite than the Asian parrakeets, but, nevertheless, they should be provided with comfortable houses into which they can retire on cold winter nights. Half-houses suit them very well, and they will enjoy the extra 'foraging' space below. I would never shut Rosellas in completely, unless the house space was really enormous. The cocks, especially at breeding time, can be ferocious towards the hens, and sometimes to their owners as well: at this time, especially, a hen confined in a small space with the cock can be in danger of losing her life. A very beautiful and normally peaceful Mealy Rosella cock of ours killed his hen when she was eggbound and came out of the nestbox. A normally tame and charming Stanley Rosella cock killed his first partner when they were shut in a small house at night; this happened in springtime, and he probably thought she should be in a nestbox. He was ferocious with us, too, and it was necessary, in later years, to wear boots, a headscarf and protective glasses to withstand his onslaughts at breeding time. His wife of many years would never ever go into an enclosed house with this otherwise model husband and parent! She did protect her nestbox however; he was never allowed in that at any time!

Aviary sizes suitable for the various members of the family are given in the chapter on Housing.

Feeding is easy for these lovely birds. Sunflower seeds, mixed millets, canary seed, small pine nuts and monkey nuts (ground nuts) make a basic diet. Shelled Brazil nuts, cut in half, shelled walnuts and hazel nuts are much enjoyed treats, Millet is also enjoyed very much, especially in the winter months. During very cold weather these birds, like all other seed-eaters, appreciate a little hemp seed, and very small quantities (approximately 5 per cent) of black rapeseed and linseed can be added to the diet during winter months. Oats and wheat can also be offered to these birds.

Rosellas will eat and enjoy the usual greenfoods: lettuce, cress, Brussels sprouts, green celery tops, curly endive and seeding spinach. It is not advisable to give large quantities of spinach beet leaves. This tends to prevent the birds from being able to make full use of the calcium in their bodies, which in turn, can lead to eggbinding, and even to rickets. Most Rosellas are exceedingly fond of the seeding heads of dandelion (*Taraxacum vulgaria*), knapweed (*Centaurea nigra*) and the smooth sow thistle (*Sonchus oleraceus*). Sweet apple is greatly liked, and some Rosellas like half an orange, well sugared or with honey, speared onto two headless nails driven half-way into a shelf.

All Rosellas enjoy branches, well washed, with the leaves removed, but the buds left. Pussy willow (*Salix acutifolia*), and hazel (*Corylus*) with catkins are great favourites, as are any other kind of willow, and also apple branches.

Perhaps the most enjoyed of all foods are the various wild berries, hawthorn (*Crataegus monogyna*), rowan (*Sorbus aucuparia*) and the common elder (*Sambucus nigra*). The flowers of the wild honeysuckle (*Lonicera periclymenum*), being full of nectar, are a special food of great value to those birds who will eat these flowers.

Rosellas should be given brown bread and milk, squeezed out and made crumbly, all the year round, and to this can be added mixed pulses (various peas and beans) soaked for at least 24 hours with two changes of water. It is not necessary to cook these, the birds seem to do better with them uncooked. The only cooked food to give, which is very much enjoyed by some individuals, is frozen sweet corn, boiled for one minute and rinsed. The luxury of corn on the cob is a special treat, which is of great benefit to Rosellas and to all of the larger parrot-type birds.

The only addition to all of the above foods, which is very necessary when the birds are breeding, is a good quality egg-rearing food. We found Nectarblend excellent, but there are many other good rearing foods available.

Rosellas must be wormed very regularly – at least twice a year. Some of them spend quite a lot of time on the ground, and for that reason are very liable to become infected with worms from beetles and ants, etc. We gave our Stanleys about ¼ ml of Panacur 2.05 solution (without additives), diluted as one part of Panacur to five parts of water. The larger species will need more, according to their weight.

Platycercus icterotis   The Stanley or Western Rosella

The Stanley, or Western Rosella as it is sometimes known, is very much smaller than any other member of the genus, and many people consider it by far the most attractive, both in character and appearance. There is nothing harsh or garish about the beauty of the little Stanley, a character of considerable proportions in many cases. In the Stanley Rosella, nature seems to be saying, 'Improve on those colours, if you can'!

The distribution of the Stanley and its rare and paler coloured sub-species *P. icterotis xanthogenys* is confined to the south western part of Western Australia. These birds are to be found in forest areas and in clearings along streams and rivers, and also on farmland and orchards.

The length of the male is about 25 cm (10 in) and the weight around 80 g (3 oz). The head, neck, breast and underparts are a vivid rich crimson scarlet; the big ear patches are deep yellow. The back and shoulders are black with a broad lacing of green, and in older birds a further 'lining' of scarlet appears. There is a broad patch of very deep violet blue on the wings, deep green is also present and the primary wing feathers are deep violet blue. The upper tail feathers are deep green and the under tail feathers are pale blue. The eyes are brown.

The female is easily distinguishable from the male; her head is only red in the front and crown, the back of the head and neck are green. The breast, in very brightly coloured specimens, may be quite red, but it is a bright brick red, rather than the pure deep crimson scarlet of the male. In less well-coloured specimens, the breast is deep green interspersed with brick red, giving a rather mottled appearance. The eye is brown. The wing stripe can be present in both male and female, but is less common in the male.

The young vary greatly in colour; no two are ever alike in the nest. Soon after they get out, however, their colours seem to merge, and it is much more difficult to tell them apart. It is a wise precaution to put a ring on the mother, because for a time some of the young will be identical with those parent mothers who are not very brilliantly coloured. For a time most of them lose the brilliant colours they had in the nest, and present a mottled green and brick red appearance. Of all the young of so many species of parrot-type birds we have seen in our lives, only the young of the Bourke Grass Parrakeets perhaps surpass the young of the Stanley Rosella for instant appeal.

One word of warning is necessary here. Give Stanley Rosellas a very secluded and sheltered nestbox, give them the same one every year, and *never* disturb the hen until she has ceased to brood the young during the day, which is when they are between 12 and about 20 days old. At this stage most hens will allow an approach. The young scream at the tops of their very considerable little voices at first, but after a while they merely consider it a good excuse to alert their parents that it is time for food!

Stanley cocks are less prone to murderous instincts than any of the other members of the genus, but, nevertheless, with some specimens it would be very unwise to attempt to shut the female in with the male; on even the coldest night an entrance trap should be left open to allow her to escape if she wishes. She will stoutly defend her nest, and will only allow the cock to feed the young after about the first ten days.

Never in all our experience have we found such enchanting playfulness as has been evident in nest after nest of Stanleys. The tricks they play on their parents really have to be seen! Stanley cocks will stoically suffer all these tricks and games for a long time, but if the parents are double-brooded, as some are, it would be wise to remove the young soon after they can feed themselves.

The feeding requirements of Stanleys are the same as for any of the larger members of the genus, and they will rear their young on the usual brown bread and milk, squeezed out and crumbled, plus an egg-rearing food. The usual clutch is five eggs, but it can be more. They take about 20–21 days to hatch, and the young start to leave the nest any time after about four or five weeks of age. The nestboxes used by us over many years, for all our Stanleys, were 17.5 cm (7 in) square by 37.5 (15 in) deep, with the usual ladder inside, and perch inside and outside. The entrance hole was rather large, at 7.5 cm (3 in). They always had a mixture of rotted wood and peat, to a depth of about 10 cm (4 in).

Stanley cocks have quite strong voices for small birds, but they are not in any way unpleasant, and should not offend close neighbours. These birds can live more happily in a smaller aviary than their larger relatives, which makes them ideal birds for those with limited space. A suitable sized aviary is given in the chapter on Housing. We have always found them most delightful and interesting, as well as colourful birds of great character and appeal.

No mutations appear to have been bred or recorded.

Platycercus eximius cecilae The Golden Mantled Rosella

This is truly one of the world's most gaudily coloured parrakeets, and one of the most popular. Newcomers to aviculture must be very puzzled when they see advertisements in *Cage and Aviary*

Birds, which often state: 'For Sale, G.M.Rs'. That means only one thing – Golden Mantled Rosellas! Although long-time aviary-bred and thoroughly domesticated birds have probably been crossed with the Red Rosella (*Platycercus eximius*), also known as the Eastern Rosella, it is the sub-species *cecilae* which is the true Golden Mantled, with its deeper gold lacing on the black feathers on the back. It is the clarity and brilliance of this colour pattern, set against a vivid scarlet head, which makes these birds so very striking in appearance.

The distribution of Golden Mantled and Red Rosellas in their original wild state is over large areas of southern eastern Queensland and north eastern New South Wales. They tend to frequent wooded country along rivers, fairly open forest lands, and also farmland, where they search for maize.

The length of the Golden Mantled Rosella is about 30 cm (12 in). The weight of the male is approximately 120 g (4½ oz). The male's head, neck and breast are a brilliant scarlet, the huge cheek patches are white, the back and shoulders are black, with the feathers on the back having a very wide lacing of deep gold, so that the lower part of the neck and the back, as far as the rump, appear almost gold 'spangled' with black, rather than the other way round. The rump and underparts are a bright pale green, with a blue tinge on the rump. The upper tail feathers are blue green and the under tail feathers are pale blue. There is a broad blue patch on the wings, and the primary wing feathers are deep blue. The eye is brown. There is generally no under wing stripe on an adult male.

The female is similar to the male but sometimes a little smaller. Also, her beak may be a little smaller and usually she has wing stripes. But sometimes younger males take a long time to lose their wing stripes, and when a female is exceptionally brightly coloured, as are the best specimens, it is very hard to tell male from female. The young are usually duller editions of their parents. The full colours are attained at about 12 months old.

The call notes of Golden Mantled Rosellas are rather more strident than those of the Crimson Rosella, but they do not disturb one's neighbours, unlike all the other birds, such as Mealy Rosellas, whose constant 'alarm' calls can be rather trying at times. The birds spend quite a lot of time on the ground, searching about for little seeds, etc. Regular worming is necessary. Their needs regarding aviaries are given in the chapter on Housing.

Golden Mantled Rosellas are willing breeders and will be quite happy with a nestbox approximately 23 sq cm (9 sq in) by 60–79 cm (24–31 in) high. A ladder must be provided inside the box, and the entrance hole should be 7.5 cm (3 in) in diameter. A perch, outside and inside, must also be fitted. Nesting material can be rotted wood, a little peat and a little compressed pet litter to a depth of about 7.5 cm (3 in).

These birds sometimes lay quite large clutches of eggs, but five is an average. The eggs usually hatch at around 19 days, and the young will leave the nest at about five weeks old. It is from then onwards that the parent cock must be watched, literally hour by hour, and the young removed to safety if he attacks them. With these birds it is very necessary to have an aviary available and waiting to receive the young. The cock may be feeding them one day and then kill them the next, so watch him!

The fact that these birds are so extremely popular speaks very highly for their rather confiding characters. They are quite hardy, but, of course, must have a comfortable house for cold nights in the winter months.

There do not appear to be any mutations, but a paler variety is now being bred, and, no doubt, with such a popular bird, mutations will occur in the future.

Platycercus elegans   The Crimson Rosella or Pennant

The brilliant plumage of rich reds and violet blues, the elegant stance, plus its hardiness and relatively mellow call and other notes, make the Crimson Rosella, or Pennant as it is usually known in the UK, a most desirable aviary bird. Although most of the time these birds would not offend neighbours, it must be realised that all the larger members of the Rosella genus can, if really frightened, give very strident calls. Under normal conditions, however, these birds have rather melodious voices.

Their distribution is confined to various coastal areas of Queensland, eastern New South Wales and parts of Victoria. Joseph Forshaw, in *Parrots of Australia*, states that the Crimson Rosella is a bird of humid forests, from sea level up to the highest mountains. These birds have been imported into the New Zealand countryside, where they are now established, and have even penetrated to the suburbs of some cities.

The length of the male Crimson Rosella is approximately 35 cm (14 in) and his weight is around 125–150 g (5–6 oz). The male's general plumage, head, breast and underparts are a rich deep crimson. The back is black with the feathers edged with crimson, and there is a huge violet cheek patch. The wing has a large patch of soft violet blue, the primary wing feathers are deep blue, the tail is deep blue above and pale blue underneath. The eye colour is brown.

The female is similar but she may be slightly smaller. Forshaw states that the female's beak may be rather smaller, and there is a slightly greenish tinge to the upper side of the central tail feathers. The young are mainly green, and get their adult plumage at around two years of age.

Usually about five eggs are laid, but it can be more. Hatching takes place after about 19 days and the young leave the nest at about five weeks of age. All foods recommended for Adelaides are suitable for Crimson Rosellas, and they will rear their young on brown bread and milk, squeezed out and made crumbly.

These birds like to spend quite a lot of time foraging for food on the ground, so worming is very necessary. An adult bird weighing 125–150 g (5–6 oz) would need 1½ ml of Panacur 2.05 solution, diluted as one part of Panacur to five parts of water. This should be given on a fairly full crop of food. Young birds should have half the above dose. Aviary sizes are given in the chapter on Housing; nestboxes and nesting materials are the same as for Adelaides.

It should be noted that the males can be very ferocious towards both females and young, so they must be constantly watched. Crimson Rosellas have an unfortunate reputation for being feather pluckers. This being the case with some specimens, it would be wise to give these birds a good powder tonic, containing the B complex of vitamins, during the winter months. Powder tonics can be mixed with the brown bread and milk which is given to the birds at breeding time and can be continued throughout the winter; or it can be sprinkled on the seed. In the latter case, the seed *must* be changed at least twice a week. The B Vitamins can cause fungus to accumulate on the seeds if they are stale.

All the larger Rosellas, and that includes the Crimson and Pennant, must be housed in strong houses and flights, with double-wire *between* adjoining aviaries, as well as outside for general protection from predators. Rosellas are best not housed next to each other. Even with double-wiring fights can occur, and the birds may also fail to settle and breed well. In spite of such problems, these birds make most attractive and handsome aviary subjects and it is noticeable that they engender great affection in their owners.

There is a Blue mutation which is rather rare. It is a handsome bird of dark soft blue colours.

Platycercus adelaidae   Adelaide Rosella

Adelaides vary enormously in colour; some are extremely beautiful birds with fiery orange red heads, breasts and underparts contrasting with violet cheeks and wing markings; others have rather dull and 'blotchy' colours.

The distribution of these birds is limited, being mainly to the north, south and east of the city of Adelaide, where they inhabit fruit-growing areas and vineyards.

The male's length is about 35 cm (14 in), and his weight is 5–6 oz (125–150 g). The head, breast and underparts are a rich deep orange-red, admirably set off by the violet blue cheek patches. The back is black with orange- or yellow-laced feathers. The tail is deep green and blue, with the underside of the tail feathers a pale blue. There is a black patch on the shoulder and a broad patch, running down the wing, of soft light blue. The primary wing feathers are black and dark blue. The call and other notes are similar to those of the Crimson Rosella. The female is similar to the male in all respects, except that she is slightly smaller, and has variable plumage, sometimes duller, sometimes more brilliant in colour than the male. The eye colour is brown.

The young are a general mixture of green and orange red. They get their adult colours at the first full moult, usually at about 12 months old.

These birds require a large aviary (a suitable size is given in the chapter on Housing) a nestbox of 23–25 sq cm (9–10 in) and at least 61 cm (2 ft) high, with an entrance hole 7.5 cm (3 in) in diameter, will be suitable; a ladder must be provided, and also a perch both inside and outside the entrance hole. Nesting materials of rotted wood and a little compressed pet litter, plus a little peat, to a depth of about 12.5 cm (5 in) should be provided. About five eggs are usually laid. Hatching takes place around 19 days, and the young leave the nest approximately five weeks later.

The usual round-the-year soft food of brown bread and milk, made crumbly, plus various pulses and cooked sweet corn, with the addition of an egg-rearing food, will be a suitable diet for the young and their parents, plus, of course, their usual seeds, greenfoods and fruits, which are given on page 55.

Adelaides are fond of fruit and are considered a pest in cherry-growing areas of their native country.

There is a beautiful and rare Lutino mutation in Australia, according to Jack Ahyong of New South Wales, writing in the AFA's *Watchbird* magazine, February-March 1985.

Platycercus adscitus palliceps The Mealy or Pale Headed Rosella

The most commonly kept type of this very beautiful Rosella is not the vividly coloured Blue Cheeked (*Platycercus adscitus*), but a sub-species called *P. adscitus palliceps*. The common name is Mealy, or Pale Headed, Rosella.

The distribution of this member of the Rosella genus is confined to large areas of north eastern and south eastern Queensland, including coastal areas. It is a bird of lowland, woodland areas, tree-lined rivers and also farmland.

The length of the male is 30 cm (12 in) and his weight is approximately 127 g (4½ oz), but can be a little more. The head and cheek patches are white tinged with yellow, usually almost yellow on the crown of the head. The breast and underparts are varying shades of soft pale blue. There is a brilliant patch of scarlet in the area of the vent. The neck, shoulders and back are black, with the feathers edged with brilliant deep gold. There is a broad patch of blue on the wings of some, but not all, birds, and the primary wing feathers are black and dark blue. The upper tail feathers are dark blue green; the under tail feathers are pale blue. The rump is pale blue green. The eyes are brown. There is an under wing stripe on both male and female. The female is similar to the male but slightly smaller, and the underparts are usually rather less highly coloured. The beak can be a little more narrow.

The young are similar to the adults, but sometimes have a little red or grey on the head.

There is a great variation in the colouring of the Mealy Rosella, probably because it has interbred in the wild state with other sub-species, and has also been crossed with the rare, but extremely beautiful, Blue Cheeked Rosella. Breeders have, for many years, tried to combine the vivid blue cheek and breast colours of the Blue Cheeked, with the beautiful rich gold-laced back of the Pale Headed.

An aviary size suitable for these birds is given in the chapter on Housing. The nestbox size, nesting material, feeding and rearing are the same as for Adelaides and Crimson Rosellas.

This has probably the most difficult temperament of all the Rosellas, as far as the cocks are concerned. It is for this reason that we strongly recommend ample sized nestboxes, which are not very deep; this gives the hen a better chance of escape if an angry partner follows her into the box. It is very unfortunate that such a lovely bird should have this great disadvantage. With a beautiful pair we had, all went well until the hen decided to nest rather early one year and got eggbound in a cold spell. The cock promptly killed her.

Four to five eggs are laid. The young hatch at about 21 days and leave the nest at about five weeks of age. They are, in many cases, delightfully tame when very young, but rapidly lose this trust in humans as they grow up, and are not as confiding as some other members of the Rosella genus. They are very variable in their willingness to breed, being double-brooded in some cases, and not breeding at all in others. The young should be removed from the parents as soon as they can feed themselves, which can be as early as 15–20 days out of the nest.

These birds are quite hardy, but must have a comfortable house for the winter. It is especially important with Mealy Rosellas to try to ensure that the pairs are compatible because, as has been shown above, things can go wrong even with an apparently well-matched pair. Of all the Rosella genus, the Mealy Rosella cock is the biggest 'watch dog'; his voice is rather more strident than that of the Crimson Rosella, and he uses it for every possible and impossible reason!

There do not appear to be any mutations.

Platycercus caledonicus The Green Rosella

With the exception of the rare Northern Rosella or Brown's Parrakeet, the Green, or Tasmaian Rosella as it is sometimes called, is probably the least often found in the aviaries of aviculturists. Possibly its rather more restrained colours have something to do with this lack of popularity.

The distribution of these birds in the wild is confined to Tasmania and to some islands in the vicinity of Tasmania. They inhabit forests, woodland, grassland, orchards, and even gardens and parks.

The length of this largest member of the Rosella genus is approximately 36 cm (14½ in) for the male, and his weight is around 142 g (5 oz), but can be more. The male's head, neck, breast and underparts are deep bright yellow. There is a broad band of bright red across the forehead and the cheek patches are deep blue. The back and parts of the wings are black with the feathers rather indistinctly edged with deep green. Much of the wings, including the primary wing feathers, are blue. The upper tail feathers are deep green; the under side pale blue. Some birds have a slightly orange tinge to the yellow breast and underparts. The eyes are brown. The call and other notes are similar to those of the Crimson Rosella.

The female is similar but rather smaller than the male and her throat is usually of a slightly orange appearance, thus making it a little easier to sex these birds than some Rosellas. Her beak is usually narrower than the male's. The young are mainly olive green with blue cheek patches. Often an under wing stripe is present, which is usually absent in both adults.

Aviary size, nestbox size, feeding and rearing are the same as for Adelaides and Crimson Rosellas. These birds are hardy, but, like all other birds, should be given a comfortable house for cold weather. Double-wiring and roofed flights would be an advantage, as the cock often roosts by the nestbox.

Four to five eggs are laid, which hatch at about 23 days. B. R. Hutchins and R. H. Lovell, writing in *Australian Parrots, a Field and Aviary Study*, state that the young are prone to expire in very hot weather, so care should be taken to give them and their parents adequate shade.

There do not appear to be any mutations of the Green Rosella.

Platycercus flaveolus   The Yellow Rosella

This quietly beautiful bird has been rather neglected by breeders in favour of its more flamboyantly marked relatives. Perhaps one reason is that it does not breed as freely as some members of the genus. For example the Golden Mantled or Red Rosella and the Stanley or Western Rosella. For those who have the space to keep a number of members of this genus of birds, they make a nice contrast to the more brilliantly coloured parrakeets.

The distribution of this bird is mainly confined to Victoria and New South Wales. It frequents rivers and heavily wooded areas. Joseph Forshaw, in *Australian Parrots*, states that in the wild, these birds are less confiding than other Rosellas, and move well ahead of an intruder.

The length of this bird is approximately 33 cm (13 in) and the male's weight is about 127 g (4½ oz), but it can be a little more. The female weighs slightly less. The head, breast and underparts are a fairly bright pale yellow. The throat and upper part of the breast can be marked with orange red. The forehead has a broad band of orange red, the cheeks are violet blue, and the back and the back of the neck are black with the feathers laced with pale yellow. There is a broad band of soft blue on the wings and the primary wing feathers are deep blue. The tail is dark green above and pale blue on the under side. The males generally do not have an under wing stripe, but females and young birds usually have some under wing markings. The eye is brown. The voice is perhaps a little more noticeable than that of the Crimson Rosella, but they cannot be described as noisy birds.

The female is the same colour as the male, but very often the orange red on the throat or upper part of the breast is more brilliant in colour. The young have a paler band of colour across the forehead, and the breast is usually a dull olive yellow, but this is variable. The young attain their adult plumage at about 12–16 months of age.

Usually four to five eggs are laid, and the young hatch at about 19 days. They leave the nest at about five weeks old. It is then that great care must be taken to watch the parent cock, in case he should take a dislike to any of his offspring. Should he show signs of attacking them, the best course would be to put him in a part of his own aviary, sectioned off with double-wire. He must, of course, be given adequate shelter.

Aviary size, nestbox size, feeding and rearing are the same as for Adelaides and Crimson Rosellas. The advantage of having rather large nestboxes for the Rosellas is that if the cock, in a fit of rage, chases the hen into the box and then follows her, she has some chance of escaping if the box is large. Incompatibility of partners is one of the greatest disadvantages of this species of birds. It sometimes takes two or three changes of partners before two birds are found who agree with each other.

It should be remembered that Yellow Rosellas are woodland and forest birds, so a steady supply of branches of apple, willow or hazel is of great benefit to them. This will also help to stop them chewing the aviary woodwork. Yellow Rosellas are hardy birds, but nevertheless, must have a comfortable house for cold weather.

No mutations appear to have occurred.

7

Cyanoramphus Kakarikis

Kakarikis (the Maori name for 'small parrot') have so much to recommend them as aviary subjects that it is not surprising that many more people are now deciding to keep these delightful birds.

Writing in the American Federation of Aviculture's magazine *The Watchbird*, Graeme Phipps, of the University of Sydney, says that it has been stated that there is a sky blue specimen in the Dunedin (New Zealand) museum. He points out that for aviculturists interested in colour mutations, there seem to be ample possibilities for developing many beautiful yellow and blue forms.

There are a number of members of the genus *Cyanoramphus*. Some are extremely rare; others are already extinct. Most people will only want to concern themselves with two members of the genus. One is *Cyanoramphus novaezelandiae*, The Red Fronted from New Zealand and the outlying islands. The bird is also to be found in Norfolk Island and New Caledonia. The other, *Cyanoramphus auriceps*, the Yellow Fronted Kakariki, also lives in the wild in New Zealand and some outlying islands.

Rosemary Low states in *Parrots, Their Care and Breeding* that the Yellow Fronted are fairly common in mountain forests. The Red Fronted also frequent forest land in the wild, feeding on seeds, fruits, berries, nuts, blossoms and various greenfoods. They apparently require and eat more protein than many other parrot-type species of Australia. The diet of wild Kakarikis has been noted to include grubs, worms, tiny crustacians living in seaweed washed up on beaches and the fat and maggots from dead sheep, pigs, goats and even penguins.

For those who are not familiar with these birds, their general behaviour is quite different from other Australian birds, let alone those from other regions of the world. One of the odd characteristics about these birds is their habit of walking straight up *and down* vertical wire without using their beaks – something which causes looks of astonished disbelief from other birds not endowed with this ability. Another odd habit is to scratch on the ground with *both* feet, exactly like a domestic fowl. (Some Grass Parrakeets also scratch on the ground, but with only one foot at a time.)

Those piercing orange red eyes are perhaps the key to a temperament which is aggressive and extremely dangerous to birds smaller than themselves. Having kept the Yellow Fronted in the past, I would never ever trust them in the company of other birds. One well-known breeder of the Red Fronted says he would not trust a Kakariki with another Kakariki (meaning cocks presumably), let alone with other birds.

These very friendly and fearless birds do have one rather infuriating fault; they will *not* stay in their own aviary. Day after day, month after month, they *will* keep trying to get into other birds' aviaries. This does not matter so much if their neighbours are either Kakarikis, or much larger birds than themselves. It can, however, lead to disaster with Grass Parrakeets, as I found when a Yellow Fronted male dashed past me one day into an adjoining flight containing a pair of Turquoisines. In a split second he went for the eyes of the unfortunate Turquoisine cock who, in spite of extremely rapid help from me, died shortly afterwards, of shock as much as actual damage, I think.

Fortunately Kakarikis are extremely intelligent birds, and, if they do escape into the outside world, they will very likely find their way back to their aviary and re-enter, provided they are not picked off by predators of one kind or another before they can return safely.

The Red Fronted is the larger of the two commonly kept Kakarikis. Its length is about 27.5 cm (11 in). The overall colour is dark green, paler underneath, with attractive dark blue on the primary wing feathers. The brow is red and this colour extends some way back over the head, and also on either side of the eyes; and there is a crimson patch on each side of the rump. The beak is blue grey, larger in the male, the eyes are red gold, and the legs are grey brown. The female tends to be a little smaller, with less red behind the ears, and the young do not have such extensive red markings as their parents. There is an under wing stripe.

The Yellow Fronted is perhaps the more colourful of the two members of the genus most commonly kept and bred. It is a smaller bird, about 23 cm (9 in) long with the same green plumage and deep blue on the primary wing feathers. The difference is the golden yellow crown of the head, set off by a bright deep red band across the brow. There is also an attractive crimson patch on either side of the rump. The eyes are brilliant orange red, the beak is blue grey and the legs are grey brown. The female is usually smaller than the male, and the young lack the extensive yellow on the head. Young birds of both species have pale brown eyes.

Kakarikis are extremely active birds, and so should be given a good sized aviary, about 91–122 cm (3–4 ft) wide, 2.7–3.7 m (9–12 ft) long and 1.8 m (6 ft) high will suit them very well. A house or half-house, which can be enclosed in cold weather, measuring not less than 91 cm sq (3 ft sq) and 91 cm (3 ft) high should be quite satisfactory for them.

A good area of flying space should be left clear, but these birds will greatly appreciate bare branches of apple, hazel (*Corylus*), willow (*Salix*) or beech (*Fagus*) on which to climb and indulge in their playful behaviour, which is so interesting to watch. The birds suffer greatly in very hot weather; for this reason I think it is best to give them a fairly large nestbox. One about 23 cm sq × 30 cm high (9 in sq by 12 in) proved very satisfactory for breeding the Yellow Fronted.

The nesting material used was brown peat mixed with a little compressed pet litter and a little rotted wood. The hen alone incubates, which takes about 19–21 days; during this time the cock hovers about anxiously near the nest, gets the hen out, supervises her eating, and sees her back to the nest. She tends to lay rather large clutches of five to six eggs.

Kakarikis can have problems with eggbinding, as can all birds, but mainly because they tend to go to nest when much too young. Possibly this problem could be avoided by not giving the birds a nestbox until they are at least ten months old, and also by giving them a very plain diet as far as seeds are concerned, avoiding any over-stimulating foods, such as hemp seed, niger seed and egg food, until the birds are mature.

In the past Kakarikis have gained a bad reputation for being extremely short lived. I do not think this now applies. Avicultural husbandry has improved enormously in recent years, and let us hope the time is past when people just thoughtlessly bred their birds 'into the ground'.

Kakarikis, properly managed and not allowed to have nest-boxes for more than a limited time each year, should live to quite a respectable age. Six or more years is quite normal now, and some individuals live very much longer.

One of the most endearing things about Kakarikis is the tender care they show towards their young. Their obvious love of, and pride in, their baby birds is most charming to watch. As babies, these birds are quite fascinating; their fearlessness and obvious pleasure at being lifted out of the nestbox to look at the world, and the way their parents fly to them at once cannot fail to touch the heart of the observer. One cock Yellow Fronted even fed his young while they were being held in our hands.

Mention has already been made of the wide range of foods these birds eat in the wild. They will grab every worm, beetle, slug, etc., they can find. For this reason it is most necessary to give them regular doses of worming medicine, at least twice a year, but not, of course, when they are feeding young.

We prefer Panacur 2.05 solution to other worming medicines. It is safe, odourless and tasteless. It should be diluted as one part Panacur to five parts water. (Shake the bottle; it has a sediment.) Assuming that a Red Fronted may weigh about 110 g (4 oz) 1 ml of the above diluted mixture should be sufficient. It should be given, through a syringe, into the corner of the mouth. The Yellow Fronted, being a rather smaller bird, should have less, about ¾ ml. The young, between the ages of two and ten months, should have half these quantities.

Domesticated Kakarikis, bred for many generations in aviaries, are easy to feed. They will happily live and breed on a diet similar to many Australian parrakeets of medium size. Our own thrived well on a seed diet consisting of 55 per cent mixed millets and 45 per cent canary seed, with a separate bowl of small mixed sunflower seeds. They enjoyed spray millet and a wide selection of greenfoods. Wild foods, such as dandelion (*Taraxacum vulgaria*) and sow thistle (*Sonchus oleraceus*) seeding heads, were favourites. Elderberries (*Sambucus nigra*), hawthorn berries (*Crataegus monogyna*) and rowan berries (*Sorbus aucuparia*) were all eaten, plus apple, carrot and celery. Brown bread and milk was always available, and they brought their young up on this, plus an egg-rearing food, with large quantities of seeding heads of dandelion, sow thistle, hawkweed (*Hieracium*), knapweed (*Centaurea nigra*) and wild honeysuckle (*Lonicera periclymenum*) flowers, from which, we suspect, they got both nectar and insects. As they eat pawpaw pulp and seeds in the wild, they would probably very much enjoy the pulp and seeds of melons, as do so many Australian birds; and also blackberries. Like all mainly seed-eating birds, they must have plenty of fresh mixed grit, oystershell grit and cuttlefishbone. One note of warning. Graeme Phipps, an Australian aviculturist, writing in the *Watchbird*, found that niger, of which the birds are extremely fond, caused sour crop problems. This ceased when the niger was withdrawn. A watch should therefore be kept on the content of any commercial rearing food supplied. Some contain an abundance of this seed.

Kakarikis are not noisy, which is a very strong point in their favour for those people who live in closely built areas and wish to keep and breed birds. Another most important point in their favour is that they are not destructive to aviaries.

For the many who like birds of which there are already a few mutations, and likely to be more, there are many interesting and colourful possibilities with Kakarikis. According to Rosemary Low, in *Parrots, Their Care and Breeding*, there are said to be a few Lutino mutations, of a beautiful yellow and red, in New Zealand. Then there is that sky blue skin in the Dunedin Museum.

Two examples of Pieds, one from a Yellow Fronted, the other from a Red Fronted, should lead the way to a new Pied mutation. This news comes from a letter to *Cage and Aviary Birds*, dated 26 September 1987. Cinnamon Kakarikis already exist in Belgium and, no doubt, in time these will become established in the UK.

8

Psittacula Parrakeets

The *Psittacula* genus of birds is the most widely distributed of all the parrakeets available to aviculturists. We shall only review four Asian species, these being the most popular and the easiest to obtain.

The habitat of this genus ranges from eastern Afghanistan, through much of India to West Burma, Pakistan, Thailand, Sri Lanka and central and northern Africa. Being so widespread, there are many sub-species.

Residents of lowland woodland, they feed in colonies and attract attention by their loud shrieking. They are treated as pests in plantations, orchards and market gardens where large numbers gather together when the crops ripen. The flocks thin out at breeding time as pairs search for holes in trees several pairs have often been seen nesting in one tree.

Although both body and tail sizes vary, there are two characteristics common to the genus. These are, first, the wide black feathers immediately under the beak, looking like a moustache, but thinning out and curving upwards around the neck. In some species they stop short here to blend in with another colour. In most species the appearance given is that of a ring, and it is from this peculiar feature that the name 'Ringneck' arose. Although this is the name commonly used, Forshaw, in *Parrots of the World*, refers to the most common species as Rose Ringed.

The other feature is a long, graduated tail, with a very long, narrow pair of centre feathers, which have often led to them being called 'Long Tailed Parrakeets'. This description really ought not to be used as there is a distinct species named the Long Tailed Parrakeet (*Psittacula longicauda*), which is resident in the Malay Peninsula and the surrounding islands.

All *Psitticulas* need good sized aviaries. As will be seen under the individual descriptions, temperaments vary, as does the propensity for chewing woodwork, but the most important aviary consideration is the possibility of an unacceptable noise factor. Most written material states how very noisy all the birds of the genus are, but this is not always the case. Certainly, if the birds cannot be visited very often and something unforeseen happens, such as a stranger or a cat appearing, they will fly onto the flight wires and give out penetrating shrieks. However, if visited frequently by their owners, having been handled when young, or hand-fed, and having become fairly tame, they will be much steadier. Any noise they make will more likely be at specific periods only, and therefore quite tolerable.

So do not reject, out of hand, the keeping of these lovely and very intelligent birds. Find out all you can about the history and background of the particular birds that you may be interested in. The best way to acquire birds will be from well-known breeders, members of a parrot society or your local foreign bird club.

For all of these species seed and fruit are the main items of diet, but nuts, vegetables, greenfoods and some seeding wild flowers will also be greatly appreciated. All these birds need branches of willow (*Salix*), apple, hazel (*Corylus*) or beech (*Fagus*) to chew. These will not only help to keep them busy, happy and in good condition, but can also help to keep the powerful beaks of the larger members of the family away from any exposed woodwork in their aviaries. Twigs and branches, without leaves, but with the buds left in place, will be especially enjoyed.

All members of the genus should be given a wide selection of seeds and nuts, peanuts (ground nuts), pine nuts, shelled hazel and walnuts, and quartered Brazil nuts, all items which will make a welcome addition to the birds' basic diet of mixed sunflower seeds, oats and wheat, with mixed millet and canary seeds given in a separate container. Safflower is added by some breeders, but as all the same vitamins and amino acids contained in this bitter-tasting seed are present in greater quantity in the sweeter-tasting sunflower, we see no point in its use. M. Mandeville, recording his success in breeding the Moustached Parrakeet, in the UK Parrot Society magazine of September 1987, writes that he gave his birds, in addition to many other foods, pearl barley, buckwheat, paddy rice and chillies.

A separate bowl of soft food should be given to the birds, fresh daily, and twice daily when they are breeding and during hot summer weather. This soft food can be made up from brown bread, made soft and crumbly with milk, and various peas and beans. Sweet corn should also be added, particularly when young are being reared, and at this time a good brand of egg-rearing food should also be given. Pulses should be soaked in water for at least 24 hours, changing the water twice. Frozen sweet corn should be boiled for one minute and rinsed.

A regular supply of soft food is very important; it adds variety to the diet, and at breeding time it will make all the difference to successful rearing because by then the birds will be used to taking it. At this time the quantity will need to be increased. It is not uncommon to hear of birds refusing to take soft food which is only given at rearing time, for the simple reason that they are not used to it.

Pieces of carrot, celery and a quarter of sweet apple should be given daily. We secure these on a pair of headless nails partially driven into a convenient position in the woodwork, or into a perch. Many birds will enjoy pear and most look forward to the occasional pomegranate, or half-orange laced with sugar or honey. Greenfood should be given daily, although not in large quantities. For a pair of birds we secure a small handful across a perch, using thin-gauge wire. All the usual vegetables can be offered as available; spring greens, Brussels sprouts, lettuce, endive, seeding spinach, green celery tops, and land cress. If wild food is collected, be absolutely sure that there is no possibility of it having been chemically sprayed; hedgerows and verges are not immune these days. Many birds are exceptionally fond of the seeding heads of dandelion (*Taraxacum vulgaria*), sow thistle (*Sonchas oleraceus*) and knapweed (*Centaurea nigra*). We used to collect chickweed but stopped when it was discovered that worm eggs can be attached in this. Berries such as elderberry (*Sambucus nigra*), hawthorn (*Crataegus monogyna*) and rowan (*Sorbus aucuparia*) will all be appreciated. Some individuals will enjoy the flowers of the wild honeysuckle (*Lonicera periclymenum*) and few can resist the catkins and buds of the hazel (*Corylus*).

Mixed grit, oystershell and limestone grit should also be available and frequently renewed. Clean cuttlefishbone must always be present, well secured on a pair of nails.

All members of the *Psittacula* genus must be wormed at least twice a year. Unfortunately, there is still a big mortality rate due to worms. We do not advise using a mixture added to the drinking water; if there is any taste it will not be drunk and, even if tasteless, how can you know if sufficient has been taken? It is much better to be sure, by catching the birds and giving the worming medicine orally. We do not use a catheter or a tube on the end of a syringe, but give the required dose into the side of the mouth from a syringe only. Panacur is recommended, and, as an example a Moustached or Pink Breasted Parrakeet weighing 5½ oz (200 g) should be given a dose of 1½ ml of Panacur 2.05 solution, without additives, as one part of neat Panacur mixed with five parts of water.

Psittacula eupatria   Alexandrine

Often known as the Greater Rose Ringed Parrakeet, these birds are similar to, but much larger than, the Indian Ringnecks, and have very large beaks. Years ago a few were kept in cages because of their talking ability. Although a fair number of wild-caught specimens are advertised from time to time, at quite reasonable prices, they are not widely kept in aviculture. This is probably because of the total destruction of the aviary woodwork that can be caused by those large beaks.

There has not been a great deal of success in breeding in captivity; the best records are those issued by the UK Parrot Society. Their breeding register for 1985 shows a total of only 58 between 1976 and 1981, with nine in 1984. It could well be that it is difficult to breed from wild-caught birds. George A. Smith, the well-known veterinarian, states in *Lovebirds and Related Parrots* that this species are notorious for infertile clutches of eggs. So breeding still remains a challenge for those who like these very intelligent birds. Those who breed from domestically bred stock record better results. These birds also seem to be less noisy, but they are still expert chewers and destroyers of woodwork.

The general look of the male is of a very large Indian Ringneck. He is green with a blue grey suffusion on the cheeks and back of the neck, and a dull red patch on the wings. There is a thin, straight black stripe between the eyes and the nostrils. The neck ring is black and wide under the beak and tapers up around the neck to blend in with a broad pink ring around the back of the neck. The under tail feathers are graduated, with the upper two being very long. They are yellow underneath and also tipped with yellow. The beak is red in colour and very large. The overall length is between 50–58 cm (20–23 in). The average weight is 255 g (9 oz).

The female is similar in colour to the male. She has the dull red patch on the wings, but does not have the neckrings or stripe, and has shorter central tail feathers.

The young are similar in appearance to the females. Adult plumage is obtained at the third moult. It is possible to identify cocks at an earlier stage by their longer tail feathers.

Because of their destructive capabilities, these birds are usually kept in metal or heavily protected wooden aviaries. It is their nature to chew and they should be given a plentiful supply of branches, with a varied diet to keep them in good condition. Nestboxes need to be large and of a thick material, with inside measurements of 25 × 25 cm (10 × 10 in) and 91 cm (3 ft) deep. Fill these up to 7.5 cm (3 in) with rotted wood, and include some small chunks for the birds to chew up.

Eggs are laid from the middle of February to early March. The average number in the clutch is three to four, and the time taken to hatch is usually 28 days. Precautions against frostbite need to be taken, as with all the *Psittacula* genus. As with the other species, do not inspect the nestbox until the hen has left to feed.

Yellow and Blue mutations, both of recessive inheritance, have been known in the past. Their numbers are very limited and thus not generally available.

Psittacula krameri manillensis Indian Ringnecks

The Indian Ringneck is one of the very first birds to have been recorded in history, both in writing and in picture form. The Romans found them to be popular and intelligent pets, and many were brought back from Asia and later taken to Egypt, Africa and Europe. Many people throughout history have prized these birds as family pets. Taken from the nest and hand-reared, they become very tame and soon learn to talk.

Among aviculturists, they are now regarded as birds to be kept only in fairly large aviaries, the prized aspect now being the acquisition of one or more of the beautiful and expanding range of colour mutations. There are a number of sub-species and, although there is some slight change in colour, the major difference is in size. These sub-species are not referred to here, as it is *P. krameri manillensis* which is the most widespread and readily available Ringneck.

A bird of elegant proportions, the overall appearance of the plumage is of a light green colour with a yellowish suffusion on the underparts. The under tail feathers are graduated, with two upper tail feathers extending to twice the length of the others, and being very long and narrow, bluish, and tipped with a yellowish-green. There is a narrow black pencil line running straight between the eyes and nostrils. Below the beak is the broad black stripe, curving down and then tapering upwards to encircle the neck in a thin line above a rose pink collar, the area above being suffused with blue. The eye is black, ringed with pale yellow. The upper mandible is dark red and the lower is black. Legs and feet are grey.

The average weight is 114 g (4 oz) and the overall length between 37.5–42.5 cm (15–17 in), half of which is the long tail.

The females are generally green in appearance. They do not have the rose pink collar and there are no black markings on the chin or cheeks, but there is a yellowish collar around the back of the head. The pencil line between eyes and nostrils is indistinct. The central tail feathers tend to be shorter than those of the cocks and are washed with blue. The bill is black.

The young are similar in appearance to the females, and it usually takes up to two years, or the third moult, for adult plumage to be acquired so that they can be sexed with certainty. Some breeders with a lot of experience, and close study of their breeding, can make an early assessment of the sexes, but it is not easy and gives rise to plenty of discussion. If you wish to make sure, have your birds surgically sexed, which can be done after they are five months old.

For successful breeding compatibility is essential. The hens are usually dominant and the cocks very wary, although sometimes, when breeding, this situation can be reversed. Do not expect any results if birds are paired together just before breeding time, which is February–March in the UK. There are, of course, always exceptions, but it is much wiser to pair up well before, say in June or July, to anticipate success.

When obtaining birds, try to find out about the conditions under which they were kept and bred, as following the same pattern and using a similar nestbox will most likely lead to success.

The inside measurement of the nestbox should be approximately 23 × 23 cm (9 × 9 in) and at least 61 cm (24 in) deep. To make it as comfortable as possible during the cold time of year when it will be used, choose, or make one from, thick material. Fill it to about 7.5 cm (3 in) deep with rotted wood, and include some small pieces to be chewed up. Do not moisten the material. It is better to be dry as the hen will take care of the humidity. Hens take a greater interest in the nestbox than the cocks and will often sleep there, sometimes accompanied by the cock, so the box should be left permanently in position.

There is no set pattern with the cocks; many will sleep out, so if the boxes are placed in the flight, precautions should be taken to reduce the risk of frostbite to their toes. Cover and protect all flight and flight roof panels and make sure that the roosting perches are of a large diameter, so that the feet will be in complete contact with the perch and can be well covered by the body feathers.

Eggs can be laid from the end of February to early March. The average number in a clutch is four to five. Incubation usually begins when the clutch is complete, and the young hatch in 24 days. The young will leave the nest in approximately seven weeks.

Do not inspect the nest when the hen is present; wait until the time each day when she leaves. It is better if inspection can take place through the back of the nestbox outside the flight, as then the possibility of causing disturbance in the flight is less.

Colour variations have been known to evolve in the wild for hundreds of years; it is not a common occurrence, but more seem to have survived, and so be seen and caught than of other species of birds. The very beautiful mutation colours have made them much sought-after by wealthy collectors in their native land; they were not used in the past for breeding, but kept in cages as exotic ornaments. With a greater knowledge of the genetics involved, there is now an expansion into many more new varieties, and, although there has been a slow reduction of cost in the 1980s, the popularity of and interest in these mutations will ensure that high prices are still commanded in the immediate future.

In the Lutino (sex-linked inheritance) the yellow colour replaces the green of the normal bird. This is an outstanding shade, being a lovely, completely buttercup yellow. The cock has a rose-coloured neck ring, with a fainter white ring. The eyes are pink and the beak is red. The hen is the same except that she does not have a neck ring, although sometimes indentations in the feathers around the neck give a faint appearance of a ring. A mutation colour is usually mated to a split.

The existence of the Lutino has been known for over 200 years in India, but it appears that they were so prized that few found their way out of the country. It was not until the 1950s that wild-caught specimens began to be bred by aviculturists. Over the last 25 years they have been bred in increasing numbers in the UK, Europe and the USA, and are now freely available.

In the Blue (recessive inheritance), a most lovely overall powder blue replaces the green of the normal bird. The cock has a grey neck ring edged with white. Both eye and beak are red. The hen is the same but does not have the neck ring. Appearing much later than the Lutino, the Blue is the most sought-after mutation, and, not being freely available, commands a high price. Sheldon Dingle in his article 'A Touch of Class or Blue for You' in the AFA *Watchbird* states that during the 1920s two Blues were kept in cages made of gold by Mr M.G. Maheck in Calcutta.

One of the earliest reports of Blues is recorded by the famous aviculturist Edward J. Boosey in *Foreign Bird Keeping*. He tells how a friend, stationed in India during World War 2, had been observing a nest of normal birds and wrote to tell of his excitement of seeing a young Blue emerge from the nest with three normals.

It has been the custom for Blues to be paired with splits, but they are now increasingly being mated with some of the more recent mutations to increase the variety.

A number of people worldwide are now specialising in the breeding of mutations. Many new combinations of colours are being bred, and will continue to occur while the interest and high prices asked prevail.

As so few are available, they are not described here, but the list includes:

Albinos	Grey
Cinnamons	Pied
Cinnamon Blues	Blue Pied
Cinnamon Yellow Heads	White Headed Pied

Psittacula alexandri fasciata Moustached (or Pink Breasted)

These birds have been kept in captivity for hundreds of years. In India they were often preferred to Ringnecks, as they were steadier in cages. In aviculture there are records of breeding in Europe before 1900. The first reports from the USA were in 1929, but none were reported to have been bred in the UK until 1953. There are a number of sub-species, the differences being slight variations in colour and size. The above species is the one that has been regularly imported. They are not widely kept and very few have been bred.

We think that they are very underestimated as birds to keep, as their appearance is most attractive and they are very intelligent. Unfortunately, they have a reputation, not always justified, of being noisy and great chewers of woodwork. This is probably due to the fact that most of the birds available are imported and have been caught in the wild. Their ages will be unknown, they will have been stressed and will find it difficult to acclimatise in an aviary, and so they screech. But very young, or aviary-bred, birds will soon become confident and these do not cause the same problems as wild-caught adults.

The pair we have are not noisy at all, making only an occasional call in a low voice that no one could complain about. To prevent them from chewing the aviary woodwork, a plentiful supply of branches is necessary. We found our birds to be so intelligent that, after a few 'tickings off', they stopped biting the woodwork. Their coloration is so attractive we think it is a pity that they are called Moustached, Pink Breasted is much the better name for these lovely birds. As the supply of those bred domestically increases, we feel sure that their popularity as aviary birds will grow.

The wings and back of the cock are light green, often suffused with pale yellow on the lower parts. The flight feathers are tinged with yellow on the outer edges. On the front of the bend of the wing, by the shoulder, there is a short narrow line of pale yellow feathers. A wide black mark underneath the beak, and extending half-way round the neck, gives the 'moustached' appearance. A well-defined thin black stripe runs from the eyes to the nostrils. The colour of the breast extending below the moustache is a lovely salmon pink, blending into the abdomen, which is green suffused with blue. The head is blue grey, suffused with pink at the back and sides, forming the effect of a ring as it joins the green body colour at the back. The two long narrow central tail feathers are blue-green tipped with yellowish-green; the under side is yellow. The upper mandible is red and the lower black. The eyes are black, ringed with yellow and the legs are greenish-grey.

The average overall length is 33–38 cm (13–15 in). The average weight is 113 g (4 oz).

In the female the main differences are in the beak, which is entirely black, and in the extension of the pink of the breast into a stripe following the line of the moustache half-way up around the neck. The head is of a lighter and bluer shade than the cock's, and the breast colour is a lighter shade of pink.

The young of both sexes look alike in the nest, being green with pale red beaks. The beaks darken after two to three weeks, and turn black soon after the young leave the nest. The beak of the young cock will eventually turn from black to red. The time factor for this seems to be variable, and could take two years or until after the second moult.

Breeding takes place early in the year, so, as with all other *Psittacula*, precautions need to be taken against frost. Nestboxes should be in position by the end of February, placed in the house, in the hope that the birds will go into them. These birds do not like to be disturbed, so if the box has to be placed in the flight, this must not be put where people passing by could upset the birds. The nestbox should be made of a thick material with inside measurements of 20 × 20 cm (8 × 8in) and 61 cm (2 ft) deep. Fill it up to 7.5 cm (3 in) deep with dry rotted wood, and include some small pieces to be chewed up.

Eggs can be laid from early to late March. The average clutch is three, and the time until hatching is between 26 and 28 days.

There do not appear to be any mutations on record.

Psittacula cyanocephala Plum Headed

Smaller than the Indian Ringnecks and of elegant proportions, with a nice disposition, Plum Headed Parrakeets have been kept in captivity for hundreds of years. The first breeding in Europe was recorded in 1880.

Being very colourful and quiet most of the time, they are popular aviary birds which do not cause any problems, especially at breeding time. They will live amicably with other birds, such as finches and cockatiels, but a pair would have to be kept by themselves at breeding time. It must be noted that some hens are extremely aggressive at times.

We had a cock who, being unable to get on with his hen, was placed with a colony of cockatiels. He was so happy in this situation that he remained there for over two years, before having to be moved because he upset the cockatiels by trying to feed their young. Those birds which we have kept have not attempted to destroy any woodwork.

The body colour of the male is green, yellowish on the underparts and mantle. The head is deep red, suffused with purple on the lower cheeks and, at the back, underneath the beak, a band of black tapers down and then up and around the neck, in a thin black ring edged with a broader band of blue green. There is a dark red patch on the wings, the central tail feathers are long and blue, tipped with white. The upper mandible is orange yellow and the lower is brownish-black. The eyes are black, ringed with a yellowish-white, and the legs are greenish-grey. The average overall length is 33 cm (13 in) and the average weight is 85 g (3 oz).

The body colour of the female is similar to that of the male, but there is no red wing patch. The head is of quite a different colour, being a dull bluish-grey. There is no black ring around the neck, but a yellow diffusion following the head colour gives the appearance of a broad ring. The tail feathers are similar but a little shorter than those of the male. The upper beak is pale yellow and the lower is grey.

The young are of an overall dull green colour with pale yellow beaks. At the first moult the head colour of both males and females turns to a light grey. Full plumage is obtained after approximately two years, at the second moult. As males tend to display well before this time, close observation can often identify them.

As with the other *Psittacula* species breeding takes place early in the year in the UK; but not quite as early as with the Indian Ringnecks. The Plum Headed generally come into breeding condition by the end of February when the nestboxes should be put into position. Nestboxes should be of a material at least 2.5 cm (1 in) thick, with inside measurements of 20 × 20 cm (8 × 8 in) and 45 cm (18 in) deep. Fill this up to 7.5 cm (3 in) with dry rotted wood, with a few large pieces to be chewed up. Eggs are usually laid towards the end of March. Clutches average four and they take about 23 days to hatch.

Cold weather can cause problems, so it is much better to have the nestbox positioned inside the house. There could, however, still be difficulties as the hens tend to leave the young alone in the nest after about ten days. It is this aspect which has probably caused poor breeding results. M. Mandeville overcame the problem and achieved success by adding an extension to the bottom of the nestbox and fitting a 60-W electric light bulb just under the floor, fitting the wires in conduit. He wrote an interesting article on this, complete with a diagram, in the magazine of the UK Parrot Society, Vol. XXI, July 1987. Although any heat is obviously a great help, an aviary with a well-insulated roof and good all round protection against cold winds should enable breeding success in the normal weather of March and April.

Past records tell of the existence of very few colour mutations. Some Yellows, Green Yellows and Blues have been mentioned, however they are not available at present, but may well be developed in the future.

Psittacula roseata   Blossom Headed

Although a separate species the Blossom Headed are closely related to the Plum Headed, and, as their requirements are exactly the same, they have been included with them.

A little smaller than the Plum Headed, being the smallest of the Ringnecks, the main difference in their appearance is the colour of the head. That of the male is a pastel pink, from which its name is derived, the crown and nape being purple. The head of the female is blue grey. Both males and females have the red wing patches, and the tail feathers are tipped with yellow.

9
Colour Mutations – Guidelines for Breeding

Newcomers to the hobby are very often fascinated by the exotic colours shown in many mutations. There are two schools of thought on these mutations; many aviculturists prefer the natural colours of birds found in the wild, and consider that this purity should be maintained, and not influenced in aviculture by the breeding of colour mutations. Nevertheless, there are very many who like the unusual and beautiful coloration and whose ambition it is to own and breed such birds. A good example here is the popularity of both the Lutino (yellow) and the Blue Indian Ringnecks.

The price of such birds is very much more than that of the normals – a great many times more if the mutation is new or has a rarity value, and well outside the prices we expect to be paid for our popular parrakeets.

There is, however, one avenue into breeding mutations that causes a lot of interest and discussion. This is the availability, at much lower prices, of splits. A split is a bird of normal colour and appearance, which carries (hidden) a gene that has mutated, that is, which has changed permanently from the normal to a different colour, which will enable the colour mutation to be produced if the correct decision is made in choosing a mate for this bird.

How to pair up a split is not understood by most newcomers and far too many frustrations are experienced through believing that mating and breeding with a normal bird would produce at least a few young of the unusual colour.

It is rare for the normal type of advertisements for splits to state that the mutations are sex-linked, recessive (autosomal) or dominant. The breeder and seller of only a few birds may well not know this information, but it is important. The specialist breeders will know, and will give this information upon request, and also advise on a choice of mating. As an example, many people new to mutations are not aware that in sex-linked colours, hens cannot be split.

An elementary knowledge of genetics is not difficult to acquire, and learning a few of the simple basic facts which are equally applicable to all of the species, will extend one's interest, enable discussion, and offer success in selections for breeding. At the end of this chapter brief explanations of the basic facts of colour inheritance are given. Read a few times, and inwardly digested, this should enable the newcomer to avoid disappointments.

For easy reference, the following schedules give a selection of mating and breeding expectations. They are equally applicable to any of the species, but remember that the results projected are based on averages over a number of nests. Intended as a useful guide to newcomers, the schedules are limited to the more freely available sex-linked and recessive mutations.

The examples are of birds of one colour mutation only. Birds can be of more than one colour, or split for more than one colour mutation. No reference is made to these or to the dominant colour strains, as this would enter into a specialised field, requiring more than elementary knowledge. For this same reason, examples are not given of the results of mating sex-linked to recessive mutations.

Pairing of Sex-Linked Mutations

With this form of inheritance hens cannot be split.

Cock	Hen	Offspring
split	normal	cocks, half normal, half split
		hens, half mutations, half split
normal	mutation	cocks, all split
		hens, all normal
split	mutation	cocks, half mutations, half split
		hens, half mutation, half normal
mutation	normal	cocks, all split
		hens, all mutation

| mutation | mutation | cocks, all mutation |
| | | hens, all mutation |

Pairing Recessive (Autosomal) Mutations

With this form of inheritance, both the cocks and hens can be split.

Cock	Hen	Offspring
split	normal	cocks, half normal, half split
		hens, half normal, half split
normal	split	cocks, half normal, half split
		hens, half normal, half split
split	split	both cocks and hens half split
		a quarter normal and a quarter
		mutation
mutation	normal	all cocks and hens split
normal	mutation	all cocks and hens split
mutation	mutation	all cocks and hens mutations

It is important to remember that all birds that are split look exactly the same as normals; visually there is no difference. Therefore, when a mating can produce both normals and splits, the difference cannot be seen, and can only be ascertained by selective breeding. This is how 'possible splits' come to be advertised, and to buy such birds is obviously a gamble.

The following table gives the colour inheritance of the better known and most popular mutations.

Genus	Mutation	Genetic Inheritance
Grass Parrakeets (*Neophemas*)		
Bourke		
	Fallow	recessive
	Rosa	sex-linked
	Yellow	recessive

Splendid

	Blue	recessive
	Cinnamon	sex-linked

Turquoisine

	Fallow	recessive
	Pied	sex-linked
	Yellow	recessive

The Red Bellied and Red Fronted of this species are not mutations. These are strains developed by selective breeding.

Princess of Wales (Polytelis)

	Blue	recessive
	Lutino	recessive

Indian Ringnecks (Psittacula krameri)

	Blue	recessive
	Cinnamon	sex-linked
	Lutino	sex-linked

Colour Inheritance

For most people it seems that the subject of genetics is difficult to grasp, possibly because most writing on the subject includes many strange technical terms and diagrams. However, once these are understood, and with a little persistence, it is not difficult to acquire a comprehensive knowledge of the evolution of colour in birds.

For the newcomer, who does not wish to become deeply involved in the subject, the information that follows is far from comprehensive. Presented in a simple manner, which explains the most important facts in the evolution of colour, it will, we hope, give a basic understanding, and so increase the interest in mutations.

The biological instructions that programme all aspects of inheritance are set in motion by controlling chemicals called genes.

These are carried on string-like substances called chromosomes. The genes exist and operate in pairs. Inherited from parents, they are passed on to offspring down through the generations.

The only genes we have to consider here are those that produce colour in the birds. The colour in a bird differs from that of a normal bird of the same species when something causes these genes to change, i.e. to mutate, causing permanent abnormality, and this mutation is then capable of being carried on to future generations. This does happen spontaneously in the wild, but is rarely perpetuated; there are few survivors, parents will often reject any strange-looking young, and those that are flighted are easy prey for predators.

The majority of colour mutations are controlled by two separate sets of genes, called sex-linked or recessive (autosomal) genes. These genes can only pair with their own kind, and, as they cannot influence each other, they must be explained separately.

Sex-linked Genes

These are the genes that determine sex, and before we think of colour, it is absolutely essential to understand how they operate. It is necessary to define these genes by symbols. The pair of genes which make up the sex of a cock are XX and those that make up a hen are XY. (In humans it is reversed: male XY, female XX.)

For conception to take place, there must be a transfer of the genes, and this pairing decides the sex.

The following diagram shows how the genes mix. The numbers have been appended to make it easy to follow.

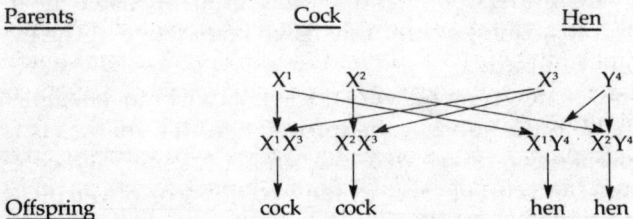

Parents	Cock			Hen
	X^1 X^2			X^3 Y^4
	X^1X^3 X^2X^3			X^1Y^4 X^2Y^4
Offspring	cock cock			hen hen

In practice, of course, there is usually a difference between the number of cocks and hens bred, but the form of evolution ensures that, over a number of nests, some of each sex must be produced.

The above diagram must be clearly understood to be able to proceed further. It really is simple. Work through it a few times, to make sure you understand it.

It so happens that the X-gene defining sex also carries the instruction for colour: the Y-gene does not carry colour, and only signals the sex for a hen.

To designate colours, let us use symbols, and, to illustrate, let us set out just two:

Normal bird N

Lutino (mutation) L

Any other colours can be dealt with in the same manner. This applies only to those that are sex-linked in the birds being considered. Inserting the capital letters in the upper case position we can now designate as follows:

Normal cock	$X^N X^N$
Normal hen	$X^N Y$
Lutino cock	$X^L X^L$
Lutino hen	$X^L Y$

This now takes us to a most important point that must be understood and remembered. The mutation colour *must* be on both of the cock's X-genes for the colour to be visual, *and* on the one X-gene of the hen. If only one of the cock's genes has mutated and the other is normal, the normal gene will override the mutation colour, and the cock will appear to be a completely normal bird. In these circumstances, the normal colour is 'dominant'. The mutation, however, is only masked – it is still there, capable of being passed on, and if the gene is later paired with a like gene the mutation will produce the colour. Such cock birds are known as splits.

Note: As hens have only one X-gene for producing colour, they cannot be split in sex-linked mutations; their visual colour must be as signalled on the single X-gene.

Let us designate a cock split for Lutino as $X^N X^L$. Using the same diagram as before we can now plot the breeding results from the mating of this cock to a normal hen.

Cock/Lutino   Hen/normal

X^N X^L $X^N Y$

$X^N X^N$ $X^L X^N$ $X^N Y$ $X^L Y$

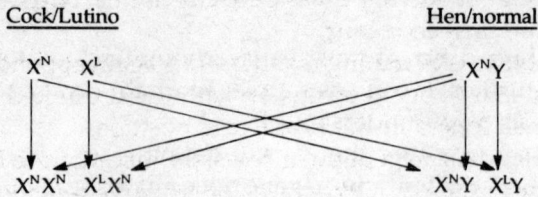

Results are always to be taken as an average over a number of nests.

50 per cent of the cocks will be normal.
50 per cent of cocks will be split.
50 of the hens will be normal.
50 per cent of the hens will be Lutino.

Finally, omitting the pairing lines, which should by now be understood, let us plot the results of mating a Lutino cock to a normal hen.

Cock/Lutino	Hen/normal
$X^L X^L$	$X^N Y$
$X^L X^N$	$X^L Y$
$X^L X^N$	$X^L Y$

All the cocks will look normal but be split for Lutino. All the hens will be Lutino.

Recessive (Autosomal)

These genes, again acting in pairs, are completely separate from the sex-linked genes. The interaction can only be with those of their own kind and they do not influence the sex of the birds in any way. Both cocks and hens have a pair of these genes, but in this case both can carry mutation colours, so we now have a situation where the hens can be split equally as well as cocks. Again the colour must appear on both of the bird's genes for it to be visual. With a mutation colour being signalled on one gene only, the other normal gene will override and mask the mutation and the progeny will appear as perfectly normal birds, but will be split for the unseen colour.

To be able to plot mating results, let us again append letters to the genes, and to avoid confusion with the sex-linked genes, let us use small letters in the lower case position.

Blue Splendids are a popular recessive mutation, so let us take these as our example. Other birds of recessive mutations can be dealt with in a similar manner.

A recessive gene that has not mutated must be normal, so we use the letter n; for the Blue mutation the letter b is used.

So we can now designate:

a cock normal Splendid	nn
a hen normal Splendid	nn
a cock split for Blue	nb
a hen split for Blue	nb
a cock Blue mutation	bb
a hen Blue mutation	bb

We diagram the pairing of the genes in the same manner as before. It is, however, more simple, as the cocks and the hens do not have to be separated in the results, as the recessive mutation applies equally to both.

Let us now plot the breeding results of mating a split Blue Splendid cock to a normal Splendid hen.

To make it easy to follow, numbers are inserted on this first chart.

Split Blue cock	Normal hen
$n^1 b^2$	$n^3 n^4$

$$n^1 n^3$$
$$n^1 n^4$$
$$b^2 n^3$$
$$b^2 n^4$$

It is seen that the results (always on average) are half normals and half split for Blue. They can be either cocks or hens. It will be impossible to tell which are the splits as they will all appear to be normal. Plot a split hen to a normal cock and the results are the same.

We now plot a Blue cock to a split hen

Blue cock		Split hen
bb		nb
	bn	
	bb	
	bn	
	bb	

The results are half with the Blue mutation, and half looking normal, but split for Blue. With this mating, and with a Blue hen with a split cock producing identical results, you can be sure that all the normal-looking birds will be split. Do not expect half of each in any one nest. There could well be more splits than Blues, or vice versa, as there will be the usual difference in the number of cocks and hens. Pair Blue to Blue and all the progeny must be Blue.

For the purpose of this book, we proceed no further into the genetics of mutation colours. It is hoped that these elementary and simplified presentations will give a good understanding of single splits in the sex-linked and recessive mutations.

10

General Advice on Care

People taking up the keeping of any birds, and especially parrot-type ones, would be wise to make a few discreet enquiries among sympathetic neighbours and local friends as to the attitude of their local governing bodies or town councils before embarking on expensive building projects. Many will say that if they had consulted every person or body who might conceivably be concerned at some time, they would never ever have started to keep birds.

Perhaps the best way to deal with this problem is to find out, as directly as possible, what the requirements of your area are, and, if you live in the USA, what, if any, are the requirements and restrictions imposed by the particular state concerned. The American Federation of Aviculture publishes updates of these requirements and restrictions and also details of any possible future legislation. It is well worth while for residents in the USA to join this society, which was, in the first place, specifically formed to fight unfair and unnecessary legislation, aimed at repressing the very natural desire of citizens to pursue the pastime of keeping birds. There is obviously no way that state laws prohibiting the keeping of birds can be circumvented, unless they are rescinded.

In the UK, local by-laws are another matter. Many have fallen into disuse, and most local and district councils will leave the bird keeper in peace if everything possible has been done to comply with normal requirements of light, hygiene and appearance. This means that the prospective keeper of birds must not, by building, take light from a neighbour's rooms. House and flights should not be more than 188 cm (6 ft 3 in) high. No building to house birds should be placed in immediate proximity to dwelling houses, one's own or a neighbour's.

No building should be erected in such a way that it could be deemed an 'eyesore'. The building must not denigrate the area, or detract from its overall appearance. It would be unwise to more than half-fill a garden with aviaries.

In the UK it must be remembered that many councils forbid the keeping of birds on their estates. Some are more lenient, but do require notice of any building to be erected. Certain private estates of houses forbid the keeping of animals and birds altogether, as do the landlords of some blocks of apartments. So, before buying a house or entering into a leasehold agreement for a house or apartment, always instruct a solicitor to make the necessary enquiries in this respect.

I know of more than one aviculturist who has had to move home after encountering total prohibition of the keeping of birds, a matter the solicitors acting for them had obviously omitted to investigate before the final transaction took place.

It is as well to remember that it is perfectly possible for a new neighbour to arrive in any area, and then lodge a complaint with the local council about birds being kept in a nearby garden. Councils are then bound to investigate, and usually send along their own representative, plus one from the Ministry of the Environment. If the birds are healthy, contented, and kept under good conditions, with adequate aviary or cage space, and clean and not overcrowded, the owner seldom has anything to fear. He or she will be told 'there is no case to answer here', or words to that effect.

If, on the other hand, the owner of the birds has, in fact, been overcrowding and does keep the stock in insanitary conditions, etc., he or she may well be taken to court or, perhaps, warned by the council and other officials to reduce drastically the numbers of birds kept, especially if they are very noisy. Similar regulations are likely to exist in other countries.

By far the best defence against harassment, fair or unfair, is scrupulous attention to hygiene, no overcrowding, siting the aviaries as far away as possible from neighbours' houses, and enlisting the support and sympathy of as many people as possible. In this day and age few people will go as far as actually taking a complaint to court, unless something is really drastically wrong.

Security

Many creatures would like to prey on birds if they could: winged, four-legged and, above all, two-legged. Hawks, owls, crows, jays and magpies strike terror into the hearts of all but the very largest of birds, more or less in the order listed. Eagles are so extremely rare in the UK that they can be discounted. Foxes, stoats, weasels, similar wild animals in other countries, and cats all prey on birds of all kinds, and untrained dogs can cause birds distress by fouling the sides of their aviaries and putting their paws on the wire. Weasels have been known to kill birds as big as cockatoos, by entering their aviary via a small drain pipe.

The worst damage is sometimes done by foxes, who, if the wire is single and not of a very small mesh, will grab a bird's leg with their claws and draw it through the wire, breaking the wire, and sinking their teeth into the bird at the same time

We have never waited to learn by such a sad lesson. We have always insisted on all aviaries being double-wired, with a space between the wires, and with a perspex or glass fibre roof over the normal wire roof.

Neighbours' cats can cause untold damage just by sitting quietly on a flight roof. By far the best way to combat this menace is to take the course mentioned above.

There is an excellent cat and fox scarer on the market in the UK, which does the animals no harm, but gives them a 12-volt shock, quite enough to stop them jumping onto the roof of an aviary again! It is not difficult to erect, and can be run off a battery, or connected to mains electricity. It comes with various lengths of cable, up to 300 m (328 yd) approximately, and is called Cracker-jack. The larger establishments selling aviary and other equipment sell the units, plus instructions for fitting.

Owners of valuable collections of birds are strongly advised to invest in one of the many security systems available. There is still a lot of out-of-date thought about these systems. In the early days a leaf or a twig would set them off, but no longer. They are far too sophisticated for that to happen now. Good ones are expensive, however, and they do need a once-yearly service check. However, when it is considered how well a really good system protects the owner's property and livestock, it seems to me money well spent for relative peace of mind. Sometimes small firms specialising in this work are much preferable to the larger and more impersonal ones. The same people come if something goes wrong. They know where to look for a possible fault or where damage is most likely to have been attempted, and can make the necessary adjustments far more quickly than a member of a large organisation, who might not be familiar with the particular system.

Transport

Normally parrakeets are transported by either road or rail. Air transport is usually reserved for birds who have to travel really long distances.

Rail

In the UK, British Rail Red Star is still the most favoured way for many people of sending birds to new owners. If it is intended to send birds by rail, it is well worth making a visit to the nearest British Rail Red Star office. There it is possible to get a special Red Star timetable for the year in question. These timetables set out approximate times for getting from the local station to almost anywhere in the UK. On the whole, British Rail is a fast and efficient way of transporting birds, provided the enquiries are made as to the best time of day and night to bring the birds to the local station. Red Star will only receive birds from Monday to Thursday inclusive, so it is best not to send birds on a very long journey on a Thursday.

Although the British Rail label does state the station to which the birds are going, it is most necessary to *print* clearly, preferably with a thick-nibbed red indelible marker pen, the name, address and telephone *area and number* of the buyer, designated 'the consignee' on British Rail forms. Whatever pen is used it *must* be waterproof.

In other countries, you should make similar enquiries about rail transport, and check times, labelling requirements, etc.

Little birds, such as the Grass Parrakeets, and the Stanley Rosellas and Red Rumps, can safely be put in a stiffened cardboard box suitable for cockatiels. However, all the larger parrakeets *must* be transported in stronger boxes which, in any case, need to be much larger. 1.5 cm ($^5/_8$ in) plywood will make a box

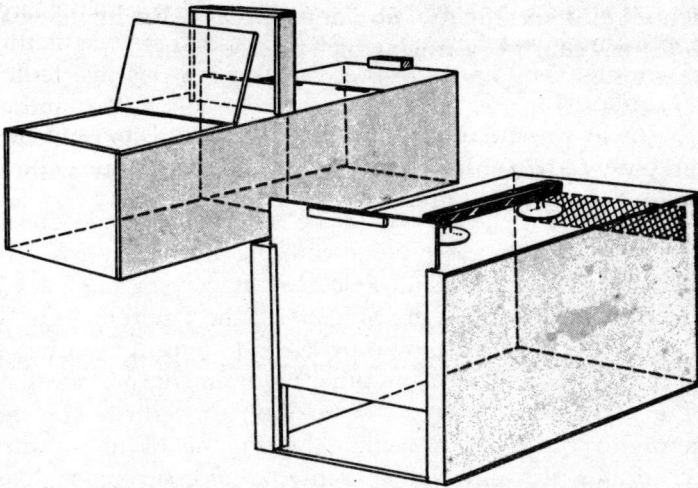

Fig. 8 Travelling boxes for use in a car. Left *a box with two sections for
small parrakeets;* right *a box for large parrakeets.*

which will be sufficiently strong for birds such as Princess of
Wales, or Barrabirds. Birds such as Alexandrines would be best
sent in boxes constructed of rather thicker wood. Small holes
should be bored in the wooden sides of the box. Some people like
to put a small window in as well. In this case it must be of a gauge
of twilweld to suit the bird being sent. Little birds seem to travel
better without a window, but, of course, they still need ample air
holes – about three to each side of their box.

I always put corrugated cardboard, cut to fit tightly, on the
floor of travelling boxes, and always give approximately three
days' supply of food. If there is some unexpected delay, the birds
will then at least have plenty to eat. Do not put water in the boxes;
it makes cardboard dangerously damp, and collects in uncom-
fortable puddles in those constructed of wood. Very many parrakeets like apple, and a piece of ripe, sweet, peeled apple will give
the birds the moisture they need. Little birds especially benefit
from having their beaks dipped in water just before they are put
in their box; that way they get one good mouthful of water before
their journey begins.

Always check that any rings are loose, clean and comfortable
before sending birds away. Any tight rings should be removed
before railing the birds. Many newcomers, and some quite ex-

perienced bird keepers too, do not fully realise the intense pain
and distress caused by rings which are too tight.

Air Transport
The best way to send birds really long distances is to send them
by air. Only certain airlines deal with the transportation of birds.

Export Assuming the birds are to be exported from the UK, the
first thing to do is to get in touch with the nearest branch of the
Ministry of Agriculture and Fisheries. It may or may not be
necessary also to contact the Ministry of the Environment. The
Ministry of Agriculture should be asked to inform the exporter
what certificates of health and other requirements are necessary
for the particular country of destination concerned. The next
authority to contact might well be the embassy of that country.

Certificates of health will certainly be necessary, very likely
supplied by a veterinary practitioner specified by the Ministry of
Agriculture. They will usually agree to a local vet, who would be
able to arrange the necessary visits to the exporter's premises.

About 48 hours' notice of the arrival of birds for transportation
abroad is usually required by airline freight departments, and, as
stated above, it is *vital* to find out whether or not the chosen
airline does, in fact, transport birds, and on which flights, etc.
Boxes *must* comply with their requirements; these are called
IATA (International Air Transport Association) boxes. In the UK
Southern Aviaries, Hadlow Down, East Sussex, supply them.

Road
Road carriers are now being used on a greatly increased scale for
the transport of birds. We have considerable personal experience
of one; it is called Interlink, and has local offices over almost the
whole of the United Kingdom (see page 145). Unfortunately, they
do not, at the time of writing, appear to be taking birds to any part
of Ireland, but perhaps this will come in the not too distant
future, thus making life a little easier for the bird keepers in
Ireland. Collection is from the owner's home, in the afternoon,
and delivery, anywhere in the UK, is on the next day, usually in
the morning, to the home of the buyer. Obviously it is essential
that the seller and buyer are available at the times arranged. It
should also be pointed out that, at the time of writing, Interlink
do *not* insure the birds. We have found this company most

efficient, and their drivers most concerned for the welfare of the birds. The method of transport is marginally slower than British Rail, and, at the time of writing, costs just a little more for the same weight being sent.

Importing Birds into the United Kingdom

Permission must be obtained from the Ministry of Environment to import birds into the UK, and an import licence must be obtained from the Ministry of Agriculture and Fisheries. The birds will have to be quarantined, and, wherever this takes place, a veterinary practitioner, either local or appointed by one of the ministries, will need to have free access to inspect the birds at any time, and as many times as is deemed necessary, at the importer's or new owner's expense.

There are ministry-approved quarantine stations who will undertake this operation for a fee. The usual period of quarantine in the UK is about six weeks, but it can vary considerably.

Breeding Records

It is of the greatest importance not only to the owner, but to all who care about the preservation of species of birds, that careful records are kept of breeding successes. On various occasions both the UK Parrot Society and Avicultural Society have produced breeding registers. These registers serve to show all interested persons and bodies that aviculture is well and thriving, and that appreciable numbers of a great many species of birds are now being bred on a regular basis in the UK. In many cases so many birds are bred from some species that they are fast arriving at the stage when, like canaries, budgerigars and cockatiels, they may be classed as domesticated.

Over a period of years, breeding records serve as an excellent life history of individual pairs of birds. Information such as the first time the pair bred, the number of eggs laid, number of birds hatched, any illnesses, and dates of worming, etc., can all be stored on homemade breeding records, or in a home computer.

Breeding records are especially necessary in the case of birds such as Ringnecks, Turquoisines, Splendids, etc., which have now mutated to such a degree that, without careful records, the breeder would be at a loss to know what to put with what.

11
First Aid

It is an unfortunate fact that a great many newcomers to aviculture take on the responsibility of keeping livestock without the slightest knowledge of what to do when things go wrong.

It is all very well to think 'there is that nice veterinary man or woman not far away'! What happens if attention must be immediate? Or if the telephone line is down in a winter storm?

It is of the utmost importance that the owner of the birds has at least a slight knowledge of what to do in an emergency. Confidence on the part of the owner, and reassurance from him or her, has given many a bird the will to live when its physical resources, for whatever reason, were at a very low ebb. Birds are mostly very resilient creatures and will try hard to survive if they think they are really wanted. Sometimes just a word or a familiar whistle makes all the difference to a bird's chances of recovery plus, where possible, the skilled help of a veterinary practitioner.

Birds found dead

When a bird is found dead on the floor of an aviary, first check to see if its neck has been broken. This can happen if a severe fright of some kind causes it to dash about in the dark and bash into things. In this case, when the bird is held in the hand, the neck will roll from side to side. If this does not appear to be the case, and there is no visible damage, it is well worth while having a *post mortem* done. That way the owner will have some idea what went wrong with the bird, and whether or not there is any contagious disease involved.

If possible, birds to be the subject of a *post mortem* should be taken as quickly as possible to an establishment which can carry out this work immediately. If the bird is taken to a busy veterinary practitioner, put in a refrigerator, then sent through the post somewhere else to have the *post mortem* performed, the chances of finding out what really went wrong are reduced. So it is really worth while to take the bird to a veterinarian who can, and will, do the autopsy as quickly as possible.

In certain cases it may be necessary to see the result of cultures. This may mean a wait of several days, or even longer. It may be costly, but is worth while if the rest of the owner's birds may be at risk from a suspected infectious disease.

Cage and Aviary Birds has arranged a *post mortem* service for its readers. The address is given under useful addresses on page 145. Birds must be wrapped in a double layer of polythene bags and put in a non-crushable box. The fee is currently £10.

Accidents

Instant attention may save the life of a bird who has met with an accident. One with a wing of a leg which is, or appears to be, broken must be taken to a vet as quickly as possible. But it must be borne in mind that not everyone lives within easy distance of help. Even if skilled help has to be delayed, or is not available, there is still a chance of saving the bird.

A broken wing is best secured with a strip of cotton or other material wrapped securely round the bird's body and tied. If this fails to hold the broken part, wrap the bird in a towel with its head and legs left free. Secure the towel with strips of thin cloth tied round the bird and over the shoulders. Put the bird in a cage with a temperature of about 30° C (85° F).

It should be remembered that the heat should come from the top, sides or outside; *not* from the floor. Nothing is worse for a bird suffering from severe shock and pain than to feel its feet getting hot. A drink of glucose and water should be given: the dosage is half a teaspoon of glucose (or sugar) to one tablespoon of lukewarm, boiled water.

In the case of a bird with a leg completely broken off, it will go into shock very quickly indeed, in fact the outlook for a small bird is not good. Such an accident may cause death from shock quite quickly. The larger the bird, the better are its chances of survival. Whatever the size of the bird, act quickly, give the bird two beakfuls of glucose and lukewarm water (half a teaspoon of glucose to a tablespoon of water). If two tiny drops of brandy can be added, the chances of survival will be improved.

Tape the broken leg with enough dressing strips to form a firm 'stump' and put the bird on a soft towel in a cage with a temperature of 30° C (85° F).

In either of the above cases, the glucose and lukewarm water should be given every two hours, leaving the bird (and the owner) about five hours' sleep at night. In both cases the bird's chances of survival will be greatly improved if skilled veterinary attention can be given. In all cases, the bird's normal foods, plus any special favourite foods, should be supplied.

For more information on accidents, see Chapter 12.

Tonics and Medicines

Two things are vital to an ill bird: warmth and water. A sick bird, or one suffering from shock, needs immediate warmth of 30° C (85° F) plus water, as such a bird is often very dehydrated.

Do *not* put tonics, medicines, etc., into an ill or shocked bird's drinking water. This will almost certainly stop the bird drinking, which is one of the things which may help to keep it alive. Medicines are best put straight into the bird's mouth. They soon get used to being handled for this purpose, and are extremely grateful for the help they are receiving. Just as with human beings, it is most important to encourage the bird to fight for its life. A word or a whistle makes all the difference to the bird's will to live.

Poison

A steady flow of liquid has saved the lives of more than one poisoned bird. When a bird is found huddled on the floor of an aviary, having been perfectly well the day before, one has to suspect some kind of poisoning.

Unfortunately, in this day and age, so many lethal sprays are used on crops that there is always the risk of some remaining on seed which is fed to birds. We know of some small birds which were lost through eating sunflower seeds which had been sprayed with a chemical which proved fatal. We ourselves nearly lost a much loved parrot-type bird of medium size through feeding Russian pine nuts which, whilst appearing shiny and good on the outside, were, in fact, mildewed inside. The pine nuts, much loved by many psittacine birds, were confiscated at once. Before too long another food giving much pleasure to the birds, peanuts, caused terrible trouble. Several birds of different species became ill, and it was pure chance which led us to B.H. Cole's *Avian Medicine and Surgery* where we read about alfatoxin, a fungal disease which is found in the ground in which peanuts grow. So out went the peanuts, and, after some medication from our vet, Alan Jones, the birds recovered. They probably owe their lives to that wonderful reviver Ovigest, which he prescribed for them, and which Paul and June Bailey of Oaklands Park Farm had found very helpful for injured or ill birds, including young hand-reared birds.

Ovigest is a liquid which, once opened, must be used within approximately ten days. It can be added to any food the bird particularly likes. I found that, once tasted, when mixed with an egg-rearing food, for example, it was eaten in sufficient quantities to bring about a remarkable recovery in a number of birds. These birds were either weak, young or suffering from the effects of the fungus mentioned above.

A dessertspoonful of mixed rearing food, or any food the bird especially likes, should be fed, mixed with 5 ml of Ovigest, twice daily. It should be discontinued after ten days.

Illnesses

These are dealt with by Alan Jones in the chapter on Ailments and Diseases. However, before rushing off to the veterinarian with a bird suffering from perhaps the commonest complaint of all, a 'knife-edge' breastbone, where the bird has a 'lightweight' feel but is otherwise reasonably well and has a dry vent, ask yourself if the bird has been wormed recently? If not, give it a dose of worming medicine, provided that it is not feeding young. Birds feeding young are best not wormed in case they regurgitate a strong dose into the mouth of one of their babies, possibly causing its death.

Those birds which have been allowed to breed too long and to rear large families, will very likely lose a lot of weight, due to the effort of constant feeding. The answer is to endeavour to limit the breeding, and the numbers of birds to be reared.

If a bird with a 'knife-edge' breastbone sits very quietly for long periods, taking little interest in life, that bird may be suffering from the disease known as pseudotuberculosis, also known by the names pasteurella and yersinia. As this disease presents a considerable risk to the rest of the owner's birds, it is best to play safe and take the bird concerned to the veterinarian as soon as possible.

Diseases caused by fungi can create tremendous problems for bird keepers. Fortunately, domesticated Australian and Asian species appear to be less susceptible to fungal diseases than birds originating from South America. Dirty aviaries and badly kept seeds, which have been allowed to get damp, can be the cause of various conditions which could develop into serious diseases, such as aspergillosis or candidiasis.

Psittacosis
See Chapter 12, p. 118.

Feather plucking

Stress, dietary deficiency, inbreeding, and inherited traits have all been put forward, at one time or another, as the reason for feather plucking. Certainly, in some birds, stress plays a large part in the cause, and an unsuitable diet would also be an obvious cause, but it does seem to be more prevalent in some species than in others. Birds which are allowed to breed when very young will thus both overtax their strength and suffer from stress.

Feather plucking of young birds in the nest is often done by the hen wishing to go back to nest in a comfortable, warm place. She is thus endeavouring to turn her young out to give herself more room! This is where a relatively large nestbox (for the bird concerned) has great advantages. A Grass Parrakeet, for example, is far less likely to pluck, or otherwise injure, her young if there is plenty of room. She will very likely lay her second clutch of eggs quite happily amongst the first-round young.

Bad feather plucking of young can sometimes be lessened, or even stopped, by a twice daily spraying of the young with a good anti-peck aerosol. But a lot depends on the species concerned. Some parents would not tolerate such interference and would promptly desert their young. For this reason careful thought must be given to the problem. If the young have been examined and they do not appear too badly plucked, that is to say, they are not bleeding, then, if the parents are very nervous individuals, it might be better to leave well alone, and separate young from parents as soon as they can feed themselves.

If young birds appear to have been grossly plucked, or even injured, then there really is no alternative but to take them away and endeavour to bring them up by hand. For really valuable young there is, in the UK, a wonderful service for hand-rearing run by Judith Nicholas and her associates, called Databird World-wide Ltd. The full address appears on page 145.

Adult birds who appear to be feather plucking may, in fact, be 'overpreening' their mates. In many cases it only happens at breeding time and usually to the hen. At other times the birds concerned may look perfectly normal.

Australian and Asian birds are not as subject to feather plucking *themselves* as, for example, African Greys. A treatment which has apparently worked very well for some pet birds thus affected is as follows. Put a knife-tip full of common salt in 500 ml (1 pt) of water daily. Apparently the birds do drink the water, and it does cure some of them. I would think, however, it would not be a wise treatment for breeding birds with young; in fact it could be disastrous in this case. Young birds need a fine balance of liquid in their diet, which could be upset if the adults refused to drink the salted water.

Any birds who feather pluck, for whatever reason, are bound to benefit from the addition to their diet of a tonic containing the B complex of vitamins. This should be given during non-breeding periods of the year.

Crossed or Curling toes

This could be caused by rickets, but it can also be a sign of lack of sufficient Vitamin B in the diet. The answer is to add a good tonic, containing as many of the Vitamin B complex as possible, to the diet. All good rearing foods contain the various B Vitamins.

Birds suffering from this problem can be helped by giving them rather small-diameter, *square* perches instead of round ones. For medium sized to small parrakeets 1.25 cm (½ in) would be suitable. The larger species will need double this size.

Eggbinding

This trying and stressful condition can effect any breeding hen, at any time, anywhere. It is more likely to happen to very young hens, or to quite old ones. It is certainly more likely to happen to birds who have not received sufficient Vitamin D in one form or another.

It must be realized that it is no use putting masses of cuttlefish-bone, oystershell or limestone grit into an aviary if the hens cannot get sufficient Vitamin D3 to convert the calcium they take into something their bodies can use. Vitamin D3 from sunshine, especially in the UK, is not always enough. In the non-breeding season the hens *need* tonics containing Vitamin D3.

A hen suffering from eggbinding will often leave her nest and sit on the floor in an exhausted huddle. Pick her up immediately and put her in a cage with a temperature of 30–34° C (85–90° F), *not* coming from the floor. This could cause her great stress because she will be on the floor and her feet will start to feel too hot. The heat source should be from the side or front of the cage. Put her on a soft towel with water and food to give her confidence, but first give her a sip or two of glucose and water (sugar will do, failing glucose), half a teaspoon of glucose (or sugar) to one tablespoon of lukewarm (boiled) wated. Repeat this every two hours, with the exception of a five-hour period in which both she and you may sleep. Remember, a sick bird is a dehydrated bird, and she will be very sick indeed until she has laid that egg.

With many species of birds, thus afflicted, over many years, we have probably saved a lot of little lives by adding just *one drop* of brandy to the sips of glucose and water, perhaps twice or three times in a day, not more. In these circumstances brandy can be a great help in keeping the bird going when she is understandably wilting.

If, after a night indoors, she still has not passed an egg, it may be a soft-shelled egg, or there may be an obstruction of some kind. She should be taken to a veterinarian, in a cage with a hot water bottle, well wrapped and insulated to keep her warm.

The veterinarian may choose to inject her with a form of calcium which she can use, or he may give her a saline douche. The saline douche is more likely to be successful with the larger parrakeet species; it is very risky with birds as small as Grass Parrakeets.

With veterinary supervision, we have ourselves helped to save the life on an eggbound parrakeet, using a saline douche prepared by putting one teaspoon of common salt in one tea cup of lukewarm water. A smear of olive oil, or petroleum jelly, should be put on the vent and then a fairly stiff tube, attached to a syringe inserted about 1.25 cm (½ in) into the vent. Between 10 and 20 ml of the douche should be injected. As it is being injected the douche will all shoot out, so the bird should be on a thick towel. With luck the egg will come out shortly afterwards. This is stressful for the hen, so she should be returned as quickly as possible to her warm cage, having first given her a sip of glucose and warm water. If the hen should suffer a prolapse, she must immediately be taken to a vet for attention.

A badly weakened hen may need to be hand-fed for several days. A thin soup of the human baby food Milupa Autumn Fruit Harvest with a tiny amount of glucose added, can work wonders. If she is tame she may eat this, suitably warm, from a spoon, or she may need to have it given to her by means of a syringe.

A bird so weakened is very subject to severe chills, which develop into pneumonia-like symptoms very quickly, so she must be kept warm and out of draughts for a week or more. Gradually she will want to return to her normal food. Any eggs she may have laid will, by this time, have been put with foster parents, into an incubator, or discarded. It is sad to lose good eggs, but sadder still to lose a good hen, by allowing her to return to her nest before she has thoroughly recovered from her experience.

Damaged Claws or Toes

Bleeding claws, or toes which have been damaged in some way, must be attended to as quickly as possible. Sometimes the loss of blood is considerable and this must be stopped, or the bird's life will be at risk.

First wash the affected foot in very cool water, then if, and only if, it is still bleeding, dip a paper tissue into some wet potassium permanganate crystals and dab the tissue onto the bleeding part. These crystals can be obtained from a pharmacy. Alternatively, a styptic pencil could be used, but the crystals are better.

Cutting Claws

Most aviary birds, unless they are of advanced years, keep their claws filed down by contact with rough surfaces such as paving stones. Pet birds kept in cages need frequent attention to their claws, because they do not have anything available to act as a file.

Occasionally, a hand-reared bird, or one which for some reason does not have much stamina, may need attention, and it must be noted that very long claws are not only crippling for the bird, they are also dangerous. Long, and often curling, claws can literally 'hang' a bird up by its leg on wire or twilweld. I have known birds who panicked so much on finding themsleves ensnared in this way that they tore off a whole claw in their frantic efforts to free themselves.

It is quite easy to cut the claws of even quite large birds if the bird is first wrapped firmly in a towel, preferably with another person to take care of the beak if the bird is liable to bite. Allow the bird's head to be free of the towel, so that it can breathe properly, and leave the feet free as well. If alone, allow the bird to bite the towel, which, with any luck, will keep it occupied. Talk to it and reassure it; after all, this is a terrifying new experience for an intelligent bird. All parrot-type birds tend to be rightly frightened of knives, scissors, cutters, etc.

Hold the bird in a good strong light and, if necessary with the extra aid of a torch, locate the quick or blood vessel in each claw. Cut each claw allowing a reasonable clearance. A cut quick will not only bleed profusely, but will be very painful for the bird. In the case of an unfortunate accident, treat such a bleeding claw in the same way as given above under damaged claws.

The best implement to use is a pair of special cutters for dogs' toenails, obtained from a veterinary establishment. These have a guillotine action. They totally fascinate many birds, so watch their tongues! Failing these special cutters, an ordinary pair of really strong sharp nail scissors will do quite well. In some cases, one or two claws may present such an indefinite appearance that, unless they are very long, it is best to leave well alone for fear of cutting the blood vessel. These claws are best filed a little with a strong metalwork file.

See also Chapter 12, p. 127.

Hospital Cages

There are many types of hospital cages on the market. Some of the old ones had heat coming from below, with a thermometer placed well up the side of the cage. This is a bad design and not to be recommended for eggbound hens, or sick birds too weak to sit on the perch. Birds could be greatly stressed, and even hurt, by too much heat from below, while the thermometer above registers something much less. Of course heat rises, but this type of cage is unlikely to be satisfactory for birds which need a *lot* of heat, but will be sitting on the floor. If a floor-heated cage *must* be used, put a thermometer on the floor, so that the correct temperature is not exceeded at floor level. A cage with the heat coming from the sides or front is best.

Quite a good temporary arrangement in an emergency is to put the ill bird in any ordinary cage, cover the sides and top, and stand the cage in front of a small electric fire, but not too close. Use a thermometer to gauge the heat, but do remember that most parrot-type birds will quickly bite through a thermometer, with disastrous results to themselves, as soon as they begin to feel better.

Nursing an ill bird, avoiding stress and giving medicine

Always remember that an ill bird feels extremely vulnerable, even although it may be so weak that it appears tame. Do *not* allow children near an ill bird, both for their own good, and that of the bird. A bird which may at first appear to be suffering from just a chill or a strained eye, due to dust, may, a few days later, develop something much more serious.

For these reasons, always keep children, dogs, cats and curious adults away from ill birds. Indirectly stress kills many birds, but I have yet to meet the cat owner who would admit this fact.

An ill or eggbound bird, one which has suffered an accident, or one just home from surgical sexing, should also be kept away from children, dogs, cats, etc. But do encourage the bird yourself with a few words, or a whistle. Remember to follow the veterinarian's instructions exactly, and on time, and do remember that an ill bird is a dehydrated bird. It needs frequent sips of warm, boiled water, with a little glucose, given as half a teaspoon to a tablespoon of warm water. The bird, whatever its problem, also needs warmth, unless the general temperature is above 90° C (85° F).

When giving antibiotics, ask the veterinary practitioner if it is in order to give the glucose and water at intervals, and also ask if the bird should have the antibiotic before or after feeding. A bird which is extremely weak will need to be hand-fed, and the vet should be consulted on this matter. If he or she does not give information on this subject, most birds can tolerate the baby food already mentioned (Milupa Autumn Fruit Harvest) mixed to a soup with warm boiled water, and given just warm. Avoid any baby foods containing onions; these cannot be tolerated either by sick or baby birds.

It is normal to give antibiotics for five days, and then to give the bird five days' rest. Sometimes this will prove sufficient to cure the bird of its troubles; sometimes it will have to have another round of medicines. There is no point in continuing to give a bird medication once it is really better, so follow the veterinarian's instructions carefully. Where possible, the sick bird should be in a cage on its own, but in a position where it sees some activity and hears its owner's voice. It is easy for sick birds, shut away, to become depressed and disorientated and to give up the struggle to live. This is where a sympathetic owner can help the bird to overcome its problems, by galvanizing its will to live with kind words or an encouraging whistle.

Whenever possible, antibiotics should be given by means of a syringe (with the needle removed). Simply put the nozzle in the corner of the mouth, or use an eye dropper.

Internal Bleeding

Sometimes an apparently healthy bird starts to bleed from the vent. Before the owner rushes the bird off to the vet, if the bird was healthy a few hours beforehand, do try giving it some medicinal liquid paraffin. Give anything from half a teaspoon, for a Grass Parrakeet, to a tablespoon for a big Rosella. Many birds, especially at breeding time, chew wood. The wood which forms part of their aviaries, their perches, their nestboxes, and especially the ladders in their nestboxes, often has a great attraction. Also, as for many birds' nesting materials consist of various kinds of wood: compressed pet litter, rotted wood, wood chips, etc., the likelihood of a hen, especially, getting some sharp bits stuck somewhere inside her is considerable.

If the paraffin fails to stop the bleeding after a few hours, by helping the expulsion of some sharp stones or wood, then the bird should be seen by a veterinarian.

Swollen Eyes

Many birds, especially those with large eyes, tend to suffer from swollen eyes. Dust in the eye can be the cause, or dirt on the perches. First wash the eye out with warm boiled water, using a very smooth soft piece of cloth. *Never* use cotton wool in any form, or any woollen or fluffy material. The eye in every living creature is a most delicate piece of equipment; treat it with great care. Any tiny fibres or threads of the materials mentioned could get into the eye and compound the troubles.

If the problem is obviously not just dust or dirt, the bird must be seen by a vet. Swollen or partly closed eyes can be a factor in various diseases, but if it is decided that the problem may be local to only the eye, then he or she will probably prescribe an antibiotic cream. Usually this requires a twice daily application.

The eye must be washed with warm boiled water, each time before the application of the cream. Dry it off with a clean soft handkerchief. Then squeeze a tiny worm-shaped bit of the cream on the lower lid of the eye. As with other antibiotics, it is usual to give such medication for five days. However, I understand that many veterinarians also prescribe a very bland cream to use on the eye during the five-day rest period. Sometimes eye problems do clear up within the first five days.

Broken Tail Feathers

A baffling condition, known to canary breeders, and which can sometimes afflict young birds, particularly Grass Parrakeets, is one in which the tail feathers keep breaking off. Sometimes they bleed, and occasionally one finds a bird which has a sort of blood-filled crust above the vent and all around the tail. A few years ago I had one such bird, an exceptionally brilliantly coloured Scarlet Bellied Turquoise hen. She became very depressed with this condition, so I brought her indoors and gave her, once a week for three weeks, a bath consisting of enough luke-warm water to come up to her shoulders, and coloured deep golden brown by Vanodine V18. This is a disinfectant used for dog kennels.

When using this liquid, be very sure to protect the bird's eyes and nostrils. Pour the bath water all over the vent of the bird, and particularly massage it in around the tail area. When the bird is totally soaked, very carefully wet the head and neck, etc., avoiding the eyes and nose. Next take the bird out, but do not rinse it, and wrap it in a warm towel with its head and legs protruding. Put it in a warm cage, or in a warm room, until it is completely dry, and try to make sure it does not later sit in a cold draught in its flight if the weather is cold. Very steady birds can be dried with an electric hair dryer.

Broken Wing Feathers

Broken wing feathers are not uncommon in aviaries containing nervous or swift flying birds. Do *not* try to pull out wing feathers; it is painful and very distressing for the bird. Cut them back with scissors, and leave the bird to chew the ends and pull out the stumps itself.

Excreta

The colour of excreta can depend so much on the temperature in the flight, and what the bird has just eaten, that, unless a bird appears ruffled and dull-eyed, a temporary marked change in colour need not be cause for alarm. Yellow droppings can perhaps denote kidney problems or some diseases, but they can also indicate that the bird is eating rather too fatty and rich a diet, or that it has been chilled in a biting wind.

The normal dark green (almost black) and white droppings of parrakeets can so easily turn to light, bright green if the birds have been eating a lot of dark-green-leafed plants. Spinach causes this change very quickly. Too much spinach (the leaves) can be bad for the hens, in particular, because it prevents the bird from being able to make use of all the calcium it has taken into its body. This means there is not so much available for eggshell formation, etc.

Very loose greyish droppings *may* be an indication of something wrong, or it may be that the bird has just seen a hawk above its aviary, or something else to cause alarm. Look at the bird's eyes and its general behaviour and, if thought necessary, then catch the bird and see if it is 'well covered' or just skin and bone; that *is* cause for attention.

Raised Scales on Legs

This can be simply old age, or it can be caused by a mite burrowing under the scales. Whatever the cause, the bird can be made more comfortable by pouring olive oil over its legs about once every two months.

Ending a Suffering Bird's Life Painlessly

How to put a bird to sleep painlessly troubles more bird keepers than is sometimes realised by experienced breeders. A bird thought to be terminally ill, one which has been hatched hopelessly deformed, or one which has suffered some terrible accident, is best put out of its misery, rather than left to linger on to the inevitable end.

Sometimes, too, there are cases where there is risk of infection to the rest of the flock. It is better to lose one bird than risk all of one's birds. Although all veterinarians will, by the nature of their profession, try to save life where possible, they will usually help the owner of a suffering bird by giving it a lethal injection.

If it is not possible to visit a vet and in the nature of things the owners of large numbers of birds cannot rush off to the vet every time tragedy occurs, the following procedure would suffice for any of the birds dealt with in this book.

It should be borne in mind that birds, dogs and children all tend to be psychic, and will very quickly 'understand' any conversation about their future. *Avoid* discussing the bird's future, or lack of it, in its hearing. Make ready all arrangements for putting it to sleep out of sight of any other birds; they will communicate fear to each other.

A bird which has suffered a bad accident, or is very ill, may appear very docile, but, nevertheless, it would be wise to wear light rubber gloves, or at least one glove on the hand with which you are going to hold the bird.

For the purpose of these instructions, it will be assumed that the terminally wounded or ill bird is about the size of a Redrump, a Manycoloured, a Stanley Rosella, or one of the Grass Parrakeets. A Stanley Rosella may weigh approximately 85 g (3 oz), a Grass Parrakeet approximately 50 g (2 oz). Obviously, a large bird such as a male Pennant (Crimson Rosella), weighing perhaps 200 g (7 oz), will require up to four times the lethal dose used for the smallest birds.

First a bucket of water will be needed. Then get ready a jug or large cup containing rather more than the required amount of Pure Scotch Whisky. Depending on the age and health, etc., of the bird, at least 30 ml should be available for an 85 g (3 oz) bird. (It is useful to note that approximately 142 ml equal ¼ pt or 5 fl oz.) A syringe with a stiff rubber tube attached may be used, but a large bird may well bite straight through this. I prefer to waste some whisky, simply insert the nozzle of the syringe in the side of the bird's mouth and pump a lot down its throat until it loses consciousness. This way more will be spilled, but it is more humane because one can act so quickly. The bird's eyes will remain open, but do not imagine that it knows what is happening after the first tremendous rush of pure whisky down its throat. It does not. As soon as the head rolls back it can be held under the water for about two minutes, until well after all spasms have ceased. Do not be upset by these spasms. The bird's suffering ceased with the first inflow of large quantities of pure whisky.

If the dead bird is to be put in a bin for collection by refuse collectors, wrap it in several layers of newspaper and then in at least two plastic bags, securely tied. Should the bird be a very special pet and burial is contemplated, do be sure to see that it is laid at least 45 cm (18 in) underground, so that its little grave remains undisturbed by predators.

12

Ailments and Diseases
by Alan Jones B.Vet.Med., MRCVS

The range of parrakeets covered by this book is very popular with bird keepers. Many hobbyists and breeders have their first introduction to aviculture through these species, which range from the ever popular and colourful little Bourkes and Turquoisines, through the medium sized Redrumps to the larger Ringnecks and Rosellas.

In general these birds are easy to keep and breed, and they are also reasonably hardy. The purpose of this chapter is not to provide a comprehensive list of ailments afflicting all the different species of parrakeet, but rather to give the bird keeper an idea of the sort of problems that may arise, with methods of prevention and treatment, and to guide the veterinary surgeon, who may not have regular experience of bird diseases, along the right paths for diagnosis and treatment.

The time involved in recognising and treating a sick bird is so critical that the observant owner, who has some basic understanding of the likely disease problems, will have a great advantage; illness in most birds is outwardly rapid when it does occur. *Acute* infections progress quickly, because of the bird's rapid metabolic rate, and a very short period of lack of appetite or fever will weaken a bird considerably. Conversely, *chronic* low-grade infections can fester within a bird for a very long time before they produce sufficient damage to weaken a bird, which will then suddenly deteriorate as if only just taken ill.

This is a reflection of the natural lifestyle of a bird in the wild. Any individual that is weak, or not performing well, will rapidly succumb to predators, and will also be bullied by its own kind – it will lose its place in the social hierarchy of the flock, the so-called 'pecking order'. Birds, therefore, have the ability to mask signs of illness for a long time, before they eventually become too severely affected to do this.

Bird keepers who get to know their birds will recognise slight differences in behaviour or attitude, which could indicate early disease problems, before they become too advanced, and therefore regular inspection is important. A quick visit of a few minutes, to push in food and water, is of no use, as most birds, except those near death, will appear bright and alert when suddenly disturbed: one must observe the birds quietly and over a period of time to spot any that are behaving oddly.

To understand what happens in a sick bird a little knowledge of basic anatomy and physiology is essential.

Birds are homoeothermic, commonly known as warm blooded, a characteristic shared with the mammals. This means that they have a high body temperature which is strictly regulated from within by various interlinked and closely controlled processes; in contrast to the poikilothermic reptiles, fish and amphibians, whose body temperature is affected by their environment. This means that when the bird's environment is hotter than its body, it has to lose heat, which it does by panting, seeking shade, bathing and spreading its feathers to allow air to circulate over the skin. Most of the time, however, the reverse is true, with the bird needing to maintain a temperature higher than that of its surroundings. The colder the outside temperature, the more work has to be done to achieve this state: by increasing food intake to provide more metabolisable energy; by exercising to produce muscular heat; by huddling together to conserve warmth; and by reducing the blood flow through the superficial circulation.

As well as these features shared with mammals, birds have many other features which are closer to the reptiles, such as scales on feet and legs, and the claws of the toes. Parts of the skeleton and some of the internal organs (e.g. the kidneys) are reptilian in type, and the feathers which make birds so distinctive are, in fact, modified scales.

The major adaptations unique to birds are the consequence of their flying ability – most of their bones are strong but light because they have hollow centres connected to the respiratory system; the pectoral muscles, which move the wings, are massively enlarged, forming the 'breast muscle' mass, which is attached to a correspondingly enlarged sternum, or keel bone. The respiratory system is well adapted to the massive oxygen requirement demanded by these rapidly working muscles when the bird flies.

There are several major differences between avian and mammalian anatomy. The larynx is small, and has a protective function, but has no part in voice production. Instead, birds have an extra organ, known as the syrinx, situated at the *base* of the trachea, where most vocalisation is produced. Considering the fairly simple construction of this organ, compared with the mammalian voice-producing larynx, plus the fact that mammals make great use of changing the shape of the mouth when communicating, it is surprising that birds can produce such a range of sounds, including some very accurate mimicry.

The most important difference in the respiratory system is the presence of the air sacs. The lungs are comparatively small, and are fixed and barely expansible, but, arising from them and their associated tubing, are several air sacs, which are thin-walled, usually transparent, membranous envelopes. There are basically 12, but these may be joined or modified in different species.

These sacs have some function in gas exchange through their walls; some function in warming and humidifying the inspired air; the interclavicular sac can be massively inflated for use in courtship display in some species, such as Frigate Birds and Pouter Pigeons; and they increase the buoyancy of the body. They communicate with hollow cavities in many of the long bones, which is an important consideration in the event of infection, but their primary purpose is to act as bellows to move the air into and out of the lungs.

There is no muscular diaphragm, which, in mammals, performs most of this task, and thus there is direct communication between the thorax and abdomen, another important point when dealing with infectious conditions.

Most of the inspired air is drawn past the lung tissue directly into the posterior air sacs, where some is retained, while the remainder then passes through the lungs, for gas exchange to take place, and on into the anterior sacs. Expiratory action forces the air remaining in the posterior sacs through the lungs, into the anterior sacs, from where it is expelled. There is a fairly continuous movement of air – there is no static pause as is found in mammals. This fact, coupled with the efficient absorption mechanism of the lungs, plus the double-action of the air flow, means that oxygen is very rapidly absorbed into the blood stream. For the same reasons, anything contained in the inspired air, such as an anaesthetic or irritant gas, fungal spores or micro-organisms, is rapidly dispersed through the system and quickly absorbed.

The features of the bird's digestive tract which differ greatly from those of mammals are the crop, the stomach and the cloaca. The former is a diverticulum of the oesophagus, and acts as a temporary reservoir for food, as well as a feeding bottle for nestlings. The stomach is divided into two chambers: the first is the glandular proventriculus, which produces digestive enzymes. From here the food passes to the muscular gizzard, which, with the aid of ingested grit, grinds up the hard seeds.

The large intestine and the ureters from the kidneys open into a common chamber known as the cloaca, so that waste from both systems is combined and voided together through the vent. Thus the bird's dropping consists of a semi-solid faecal portion, which is normally dark green, surrounded by a white urinary component. Most of the Grass Parrakeets come from arid regions of the world, and feed on a dry, seed-based diet. Therefore their normal droppings are small, firm and with little fluid content. This is in marked contrast to the bulky wet droppings of fruit-eaters and softbills.

The heart and circulatory system of the parrakeets is fundamentally very similar to that of mammals, with two noteworthy exceptions. The red blood cells (erythrocytes) retain their nuclei in birds, and are more oval in shape than those of mammals. Secondly, a renal portal system is found in birds, as well as the hepatic portal system found in both groups. That is to say, some blood, returning from the legs, passes through the kidneys before reaching the heart and being recirculated. This can be significant if drugs are given by injection into the leg. The hepatic portal system involves the passage of blood from the gut through the liver before it returns to the heart.

Having briefly described some of the structure and function of the avian anatomy, I should like to mention some of the important factors involved in the diagnosis and treatment of disease.

If you are to take a sick bird to an interested veterinary surgeon, there is a certain amount of information that he or she will need in order to make a diagnosis. There is often so little difference in outward signs in birds that may be ill from a wide variety of diseases – that is to say, a sick bird looks miserable, fluffed up and quiet, is probably not eating, and usually has loose droppings, but it could have any of a dozen complaints. Therefore, careful questioning and detailed background information are important before we even look at the bird, in order that we can get some clues as to the disease involved.

Where possible, the veterinarian will prefer to examine the patient at the surgery where there are more complete facilities for diagnosis and treatment, but, on occasions, it can be an advantage to see the bird in its own environment. This is especially true of the parrakeets, which tend to be kept as aviary birds rather than as single-pet caged birds.

If a bird is taken to the surgery, the following points should be considered:

1 Ideally bring the bird in its own cage. In the case of larger species or aviary birds, this may not be possible, in which case a transport cage or box must be used, but certain information can be gained from seeing the bird's normal accommodation.
2 Cover the cage and warm the car before the journey.
3 Remove water, to avoid spillage, but bring normal food used for inspection, plus any medication already given. Owners will often try a remedy on the advice of a friend or pet-shop before seeking veterinary attention, and it is helpful to be able to see what has already been used, before administering any more drugs.
4 Do *not* remove the droppings, or try to clean the cage. One can well appreciate that the owner wishes to impress on the veterinarian that his or her bird is hygienically looked after. Thus the cage is scrubbed and presented in pristine condition, having nicely eliminated the information needed by the vet, such as the appearance and quantity of droppings, the possibilities of blood or vomit, and other things, such as the presence of mites in crevices of the cage.

The veterinary surgeon should then ask questions such as:

1 What is the problem and how long has it been observed? How frequently do signs and symptoms occur, or are they present all the time?

2   How long has the bird been owned, and where did it come from?

3   Is this the only bird affected, or are there others? If so, how many, and what species?

4   Have there been any previous illnesses, and what treatments were given?

5   Does the bird stay in its cage permanently, or is it allowed to fly free? If so, is there any history of it flying into obstacles in the home? Can it reach and eat houseplants or wallpaper? Has the aviary recently been repainted or treated, or have new plants been introduced?

6   Has there been any recent change in the environment of the bird – has it been moved to a new room, or even across the same room; has there been any building or decorating going on, or treatments such as those for dry rot or woodworm; has there been a change of household routine, such as visitors staying; or have any accidents, such as fires or chemical spillage, occurred?

7   Has there been any change in feeding routine or food type and source of supply? If so, how long ago? If possible, bring samples of both new and old food for checking. New fruits or vegetables are often given when in season, but the bird may not be used to them. Has it been given branches or twigs from unsuitable trees to chew?

The veterinarian can then proceed to examine the bird directly. It should first be observed quietly, noting its attitude and position, looking for signs of wheezing or tail bobbing, and noting its interest or otherwise in its surroundings. In an aviary situation, watch for the interaction with other members of the flock.

Only then should the bird be held and examined in more detail, being especially careful, of course, if signs of respiratory distress have already been observed, as handling such a bird can be fatal. A very nervous bird is best approached by lowering the lighting, and ensuring a quiet, calm attitude. The smaller birds, such as Turquoisines, can be restrained in the bare hand, but the larger species can inflict a painful bite if frightened, so if in doubt it is best to use a small towel or light glove for protection. Birds in an aviary will probably have to be caught with a net, and practice is necessary in the art of using such a tool comfortably and successfully.

The bird is cupped in the hand, with the first two fingers on either side of the head, the thumb supporting one wing, and the third and fourth fingers holding the other wing close to the body. The other hand is then free to examine the bird, or, ideally, an experienced assistant can hold the bird in this way, allowing the veterinarian to have both hands free. One is aware of how much pressure is being put on the bird: it needs to be held firmly but gently, so that it is restrained but comfortable, and therefore confident. It should not be squeezed tightly so that it cannot breathe. Do not be surprised at the number of soft feathers lost in the handling process, especially in species such as the Crimson Rosella (Pennant).

With luck, having come this far, the veterinary surgeon can make a tentative diagnosis and initiate suitable treatment, but often further information will be required, which will necessitate hospitalisation and perhaps X-ray examination, or laboratory tests on blood or droppings.

The importance of *post mortem* examinations (autopsy) must be mentioned here. Obviously the examination of a dead single pet bird serves no great advantage to the owners except to prove a diagnosis or satisfy curiosity; but, where several birds are kept together, useful information can be gained, which could save the lives of surviving birds if a *post mortem* is performed on a dead individual. It can even be worth sacrificing a very sick bird that probably will not live, in order that a specific diagnosis may be made at *post mortem*, and the rest of the flock at risk can then be successfully treated before they, too, succumb. A single bird found suddenly dead may well have died from an individual problem, such as a heart attack or accident, but it could equally be the first of a flock to be affected by a contagious disease, and only an autopsy will distinguish that fact.

In my experience the commonest problems found in parrakeets at autopsy are pseudotuberculosis and worm infestation, closely followed by psittacosis. These conditions will be dealt with in more detail below.

We can now proceed to consider some of the more specific disease problems afflicting parrakeets. The important points to emphasise in treating any sick bird are *speed, warmth* and *fluids*. As mentioned earlier, a bird will weaken very rapidly when ill, and therefore regular inspection of the stock, with prompt treatment where indicated, will save lives. It is no good thinking 'it looks a bit rough tonight, I'll check it again in the morning', because tomorrow is likely to be too late.

Having identified a potential patient, the next stage is to provide isolation and warmth. Many a sick bird can be saved by increased temperature alone, without recourse to drug treatment. The ideal is a small cage and an infra-red heat lamp, which can be mounted to one side. The bird is then able to move to the other side of the cage if it gets too hot. Failing this, local heat can be provided, with a low-wattage light bulb, or else the whole room must be heated to *at least* 21° C (70° F), or preferably 24–27° C (75–80° F). The cage can be shielded with a blanket or thick towel. Once the bird has recovered, it is important to lower the temperature again gradually, and not to put the bird straight back outside into a cold aviary.

Thirdly, a sick bird will dehydrate rapidly, especially if feverish, diarrhoeic or vomiting. It can survive without food for a little while, but must be made to drink. Water is best boiled and offered not too cold, and is more effective with the addition of a little honey, glucose or brown sugar. Once under the heat lamp, the patient is likely to drink readily, but if it does not, the liquid must be given by hand, using a dropper, syringe or small spoon. Try to get the bird to take a few drops every 30–40 minutes. Suitable fluids may need to be given by injection if necessary – 2 per cent of the bodyweight can be given immediately, subcutaneously, or in severe cases, or larger species, intravenously.

These three steps, together with nursing and 'TLC' (tender loving care), will save many a bird.

Accidents

Parrakeets are swift and fairly skilful fliers, but many accidents are seen as a result of them flying into obstacles in the aviary or home. Most species are easily startled or frightened, and can panic if an aviary is disturbed by an inquisitive cat or a large wild bird. Much of this aspect has been covered in the chapter on First Aid, and most bruising or grazing injuries are simply dealt with by antiseptic bathing and perhaps some antibiotic dusting powder. Birds that fly into windows or mirrors can haemorrhage from the beak: this may be stemmed in the same way as bleeding from careless beak or nail clipping, with a styptic pencil, a little ferrous sulphate or potassium permanganate, or even just finger pressure over a little dry cotton wool.

If such an injury is severe, the beak base may start to separate after a few days. The damaged layers will peel off, and new beak tissue will regrow, but the bird will need a soft food diet, or even hand feeding for a while. Such a bird must also be checked for signs of concussion or skull damage.

Broken bones in wings or legs are common accidents, and once the bird has been treated as described under First Aid, the injury is best managed by a veterinarian.

Broken bones heal very rapidly in birds, but if a successful return to normal function is to be achieved, it is important to ensure that the broken fragments are aligned and apposed accurately. Because of the comparatively light bodyweight and delicate structure of a bird, heavy splints, strappings or plaster casts are unsuccessful. Any method used to support the bones must be light but strong, and must not be left in place for too long, or else muscle wastage, tendon contraction and joint fixation will occur, which may cripple the bird more severely than the original fracture.

Internal fixation of broken leg bones, using fine intramedullary pins or Kirschner wires, is successfully employed in raptors and larger parrots, but for the smaller species it is rarely necessary to resort to such surgery. Most leg or wing fractures will heal adequately with simple strapping, as described below, and although return to normal function may be less than 100 per cent, this is seldom of serious importance in the smaller cage and aviary birds. Severe damage to the legs can necessitate amputation, but, again, small species will readily adapt and manage on one leg. Larger species kept for breeding, however, may not be suitable candidates for such surgery, as they would find treading and mating difficult.

Leg fractures are best supported with adhesive tape or plaster, placed on either side of the limb, with the bird held on its back and the leg extended. Once the bones are realigned and the joints are in as near normal an angle of flexion as possible for perching, the plaster is secured on each side, with an overlap to front and back of the leg. This overlap can then be 'crimped' with artery forceps (haemostats) to secure the support.

Broken wings are supported by holding the wings in their normal resting flexed position, then fixing them in place with a tape encircling the shoulder area. A small tape is wrapped around the wing tips at their crossover, to provide further support and counter-balance, and in larger birds a third tape may be laid longitudinally to join the first two. A suitable tape for this technique is masking or autoclave tape, which is light but strong, and will stay attached for the duration of healing, but is much more easily removed from the feathers when the time comes than either sticky tape or adhesive plaster.

Most fractures should be well healed by three to four weeks, but it is worth checking and replacing the strapping at 10–14 days. The bird should be kept cage-confined for a further two weeks after the support is finally removed.

Tight Rings

Many individual birds have leg rings of plastic or metal which can cut into the leg and cause circulatory problems if they are too tight, or if the leg becomes swollen. These must be rapidly removed by a veterinary surgeon, otherwise the leg or foot will die because of lack of blood supply. Plastic rings are fairly easily cut, but aluminium types require a little more care and effort. They may be cut by a nibbling action with the tips of open-ended nail clippers, or there are varieties of specific ring-removing tools available, which are far more satisfactory and will remove the ring with minimal damage to the leg.

Wing, Beak and Nail Clipping

Beak trimming is rarely necessary in parrakeets, compared to the frequent problem encountered in budgerigars, but if one half of the beak gets damaged, the opposite half may require regular attention. Likewise, nails rarely become overgrown in aviary birds which have sufficient exercise and various sizes of branches for perching on, but cage birds often need their nails trimmed. Both beak and claws can be cut with care, using a small nail-clipper or stout blunt-ended scissors. The quick, or vein, is usually visible in lighter coloured individuals, but, if cut, the haemorrhage is readily controlled with a styptic pencil, ferrous sulphate, potassium permanganate, or cotton wool pressure as mentioned above.

It can be an advantage to trim the wings of indoor pet parrakeets, to prevent them flying into windows and ornaments, but make sure they are not so incapacitated that they cannot escape the family cat or dog! The procedure involves cutting the primary feathers on one wing so that the bird is unbalanced and cannot gain lift. A bird with both wings trimmed can remain balanced and can often get enough lift to fly using only the secondaries.

The cosmetic technique used with some birds retains the first two primary feathers while the next six to eight are cut across, using a sharp pair of straight scissors at the level of the tips of the coverts. This is done looking at the outer surface of the wing, and not at the inner level of coverts. This method results in a neat appearance when the bird is at rest with its wings crossed, but is rarely successful in parrakeets, because they are such strong fliers that they can manage on just the remaining two flight feathers. It is far better to cut all of the first eight to ten primaries. Obviously, wing clipping is not relevant or necessary for birds living in aviaries.

Skin and Feather Conditions

Traumatic skin lesions have been covered in the chapter on First Aid and accidents; other skin and feather problems are rarely seen in parrakeets. Feather cysts and skin tumours are occasionally encountered, and may be surgically removed if necessary.

We have seen white or yellow feathers occurring sporadically in birds with normal green or blue plumage. This lack of pigment may be the result of mutation, in which case further breeding from these birds can produce Lutino strains, but more usually it occurs because of injury to the growing feather. This damage may be physical, e.g. the fledglings are plucked by the parents in the nest, in which case the abnormal feathers are usually replaced by normal plumage when the bird moults. Alternatively, the damage may be metabolic – caused by a dietary deficiency of vitamins or amino acids during feather growth. Again, normal feathers will appear after moulting if the diet is corrected.

Habitual feather plucking, as a result of boredom or frustration, is a problem commonly encountered in caged birds. Since most of the parrakeets covered by this book are aviary-maintained, this type of problem is rarely seen in these species. The pattern of feather pulling most usually observed is damage to the head, neck and shoulder feathers of fledglings in the nest, by parents. This frequently happens because the hen bird is ready to lay another clutch, and the provision of a second nestbox, or removing the youngsters if they are old enough to fend for themselves, will often solve the problem. A useful practice is to place such early-weaned youngsters in a communal juvenile flight, where the more advanced birds will often continue to feed and encourage those less well developed.

External Parasites

These do not cause severe problems in Grass Parrakeets, but wherever a number of birds in a flight show evidence of feather loss and increased irritability, parasites should be suspected. Biting mosquitoes and gnats may trouble nesting birds in warm weather, and fleas, bugs or ticks are occasionally encountered. Forage mites will be brought in in bags of seed, and, if seed debris is allowed to accumulate in a warm environment, these can multiply sufficiently to create a nuisance.

All these are easily eliminated with the use of insecticidal sprays or powders containing pyrethrins (e.g. Willothrin) or bromocyclen (e.g. Alugan), or solid blocks such as Vapona, plus attention to hygiene in the crevices of cages or nestboxes.

Feather lice can be more troublesome, producing signs of restlessness, ruffled appearance, and continual preening. These parasites are large enough to be seen with the naked eye, and their eggs are also visible, stuck alongside the feather shafts. Since their whole life cycle is spent on the bird, they are readily eliminated by the regular use of the above parasiticides, at seven- to ten-day intervals.

Surface-dwelling mites such as *Dermanyssus gallinae* (red mite) can be a serious irritant to birds, and, in sufficient numbers, can result in debility and anaemia because of their blood-sucking activities. They can also transmit blood protozoa, such as *Lankesterella*. These red mites live in cracks and crevices in the environment, and only come out to feed on the birds at night, so they are best detected at this time by covering the cage or nestbox with a white cloth, on which the parasites will collect and be visible as red dots after their blood meal. Treatment and elimination depend more on scrubbing the environment, using washing soda followed by an insecticide such as Malathion, rather than treating the birds directly.

Conjunctivitis

Inflamed and infected eyes are commonly encountered in parrakeets, and may be part of a more generalised respiratory infection (see below), but they can also be primary conditions in their own right. Conjunctivitis (inflammation of the membranes of the eye) and blepharitis (swelling and inflammation of the eyelid) may result from irritants such as draught, disinfectant, pieces of sand and grit, or attack from other birds. These causes are best treated as described in the chapter on First Aid, by bathing and perhaps a bland ophthalmic ointment.

Infectious conjunctivitis is caused by a variety of organisms, perhaps the most persistent of which is *Mycoplasma*. Elimination of this organism requires prolonged use of a suitable antibiotic preparation (ideally selected as a result of culture and sensitivity testing of the germ), maintained for three to four weeks. Preparations in the form of drops are usually easier to apply than ointments, but the latter have the advantage of a more lasting effect on the eye. As with ophthalmic problems in any animal, where there is ulceration of the corneal surface, preparations containing corticosteroid should not be used; the protective technique of suturing the eyelids over in these cases is perfectly feasible in birds.

One should always look for signs of associated diseases when a bird with conjunctivitis is presented, as this condition is often connected with sinusitis or other respiratory-tract diseases. Birds will often show eye problems as a result of 'stress', such as movement from one aviary to another.

Frostbite

This can be a real problem in aviary birds which perch in severe weather. The toes are very small, with no feather protection and a limited blood supply, and are therefore easily affected by sub-zero temperatures. Affected toes will become dark in colour, shrivel and become stiff, and are best amputated, although they will eventually drop off it left untreated.

Conditions Affecting the Respiratory System

Sinusitus

This is a very common ailment in many of the larger psittacine birds, but it rarely occurs in the parrakeets. However, if contracted, it can be just as persistent and difficult to cure as in the larger birds.

As mentioned in the description of the respiratory system, the bird has many air sacs, which intercommunicate, and will also connect with the sinuses, which are air chambers within the bones of the skull. These chambers can become a site of chronic infection, occasionally as the result of injury, but usually in association with respiratory infection. There are many organisms involved, including *mycoplasmas*, and often several bacteria are present in combination. Progress of the condition is slow, and the pus which gradually accumulates tends to be thick and caseous (cheesy), therefore, by the time signs are noticed, treatment with systemic antibiotics alone is rarely successful in penetrating and dispersing the infection.

Affected birds have swelling above or below one or both eyes, with resulting closure of the palpebral fissure, and sometimes swelling is evident between the rami of the mandible. If the swelling is soft, the pus may be extracted by needle puncture and suction with a syringe. The sinus can then be irrigated with an antiseptic or antibiotic solution via the needle, or via the nostril. This procedure often needs repeating until full resolution is achieved. If, however, the swelling is firm because the content is caseous, then surgical removal of the plug is necesary, using a fine-pointed scalpel blade, again followed by antibiotic lavage. Commonly indicated antibiotics are Tylosin, Gentamycin, or Lincomycin.

Birds have a very high requirement for Vitamin A, and a deficiency of this vitamin is very common, especially in birds fed a diet high in sunflower seed. Lack of the vitamin damages epithelial surfaces as mentioned below, and therefore allows secondary infections to gain access. Sinusitis is often associated with mild hypovitaminosis A, and any bird suffering from chronic respiratory disease will benefit from Vitamin A therapy.

Air Sacculitis

This is a common disease in all birds, as, for reasons mentioned in the description of the respiratory tract on page 120, the air sacs are vulnerable to invasion and damage by a wide variety of pathogens.

Many cases of inflammation and resulting exudate are caused by irritant vapours, such as ammonia, disinfectants, paraffin, and cooking oil. Infectious agents include viruses such as Newcastle disease; bacteria such as streptococci, *E.coli*, *Pasteurella*, *Yersinia*, *Klebsiella*, *Salmonella*, *Mycobacterium tuberculosis*, *Mycoplasma* and *Chlamydia*; and fungal agents such as *Aspergillus*. Acute cases manifest with signs of depression, lack of appetite, and the general misery of any sick bird, but with the added indicators of a nasal discharge and tail bobbing. Most birds flick their tails repeatedly when excited or alarmed, but the motion ceases on relaxation. A bird that is suffering from a respiratory disease – either sacculitis or pneumonia – will continue to tail-bob when at rest. Auscultation with a stethoscope will reveal bubbly fluid or wheezy sounds.

Treatment includes isolation of infected birds, with attention to hygiene and disinfection of cages and food bowls, increased warmth and humidity and enforced inhalation of decongestant vapours. Tempting food should be offered, or hand-feeding may even be necessary; and drinking water should be enriched with glucose, honey, or fruit juices. Multivitamin therapy is valuable, along with the use of broad spectrum antibiotics, such as Tylosin, Chloramphenicol, and Chlortetracycline.

Chronic forms, usually associated with tuberculosis or aspergillosis, appear as longer lasting debility, with marked loss of weight, and dry rasping sounds on ausculation. There may be an audible 'click' as pieces of dried exudate are moved in the sacs by the flow of air. Such cases are difficult to diagnose in life, and almost impossible to cure.

Aspergillus fumigatus is a ubiquitous fungus whose spores can be inhaled to develop an infection within the respiratory system. The spores germinate and grow into a mould mass on the lining membranes, accumulating a caseous exudate in the process. Birds are more susceptible to infection if already debilitated, and spores are then readily contracted from damp, rotting fruit or vegetables. Attention must be paid, therefore, to the general condition of birds and their feeding to avoid the development of this distressing and virtually incurable disease. Any wasted fruit or seed should be rapidly cleared away. If seed is purchased in bulk before feeding, it should be stored in cool, dry, dark conditions, which will delay the development of mould formation, and also reduce the rate of loss of vitamin activity. Warm, damp, light situations have the opposite, undesirable effect.

Pneumonia
This is an acute, often per-acute, infection of the lungs, by any of the bacteria of viruses mentioned above, and can be rapidly fatal. Signs seen are those described for sacculitis, including tail bobbing, but are usually more rapid in onset and more marked, and without the nasal discharge. Auscultation of the thorax reveals moist râles.

Supportive treatment with heat and fluid therapy is vitally important, as is rapid antibiotic therapy. Oral administration, via food or drinking water, is unlikely to be effective quickly enough, and the bird will probably not take it voluntarily anyway. This is one occasion when direct oral administration by dropper, or better still intramuscular injection, is positively indicated. Both methods involve handling and severely stressing a very sick bird, and this can prove fatal, but, without the treatment, a bird with pneumonia will usually die anyway.

Psittacosis
This important disease condition features respiratory as well as enteric signs, which brings us on to the next section of illnesses, but it is worthy of a little consideration by itself.

The causal organism is *Chlamydia psittaci*, an agent which is like a virus in that it can only grow and multiply within the cells of its host animal, but in other ways is like a bacterium, including being susceptible to antibiotics, especially tetracyclines. It is a ubiquitous organism, and affects many species in a variety of ways, causing abortion in goats and sheep, conjunctivitis and respiratory disease in cats and dogs, severe respiratory disease in humans, and generalised illness, with mainly respiratory signs, in birds. The general condition is referred to as chlamydiosis in any species, ornithosis when it affects birds, and psittacosis when occuring specifically in psittacine birds. The latter is the name by which it is most familiar to aviculturists.

There are several strains involved, of varying virulence, and the severity of the disease produced will depend on the pathogenicity of the strain, and the susceptibility of the host. Some species, such as parrakeets, have a high innate resistance, whereas finches have very little resistance and therefore a high mortality rate.

The condition is complicated by the fact that numerous birds harbour the organism without showing any signs of illness – these are known as carriers. These individuals can begin to excrete the organism, and thus infect other birds, when subject to stress, such as import and quarantine, transportation, another disease, or a change of routine. Thus the introduction of a new bird into an aviary can have dire consequences should it be carrying the infection.

The *Chlamydia* are excreted from an infected bird in faeces and nasal discharges, and transmission to other birds is by aerosol formation and dust carried from these deposits. Incubation can vary from 4–100 days, however, so contact with an infected bird may have occurred long before the signs develop. The organism can survive for several months off the host in a dirty environment, but spread of infection is reduced by careful disposal of waste and seed, damping down floors and daily disinfection. A good disinfectant is benzalkonium chloride.

Birds which contract the disease will show upper respiratory signs, i.e. conjunctivitis, discharge from eyes and nose, blocked nostrils and snuffly breathing, plus listlessness and loss of appetite. There is usually a bright green diarrhoea, sometimes with blood staining. Long-standing cases become very emaciated.

Positive diagnosis in life is difficult, and can only be performed by specialist laboratories. Blood samples may be tested for antibodies to *Chlamydia*, but to prove current infection, compared to exposure sometime in the past, two samples are needed at 10–14 day intervals, showing a rising titre of antibodies. Faeces may be examined and cultured, but again this procedure takes seven to ten days, and samples must be very fresh for the organism to be found. Both techniques are therefore unable to give an immediate answer, but in the meantime steps must be taken to control the spread of suspected infection.

Post mortem diagnosis is more reliable and immediate; but should be carried out with care to prevent the spread of infection to humans. Gross abnormalities seen typically include clouding of the air sacs, with variable amounts of exudation; enlargement and congestion of the liver; and gross enlargement of the spleen. All these signs may be seen in other septicaemic diseases, so are not in themselves conclusively diagnostic, but enlargement of the spleen particularly should always lead one to suspect psittacosis. The spleen is situated underneath the gizzard, just to the left of the mid-line, and, in a normal parrakeet, this would be perhaps 4–5 mm in diameter. It is roughly spherical, and should be a rich red-brown in colour. A spleen infected with *Chlamydia* enlarges to three or four times its normal size, and may appear dark and congested, or mottled.

A more precise confirmation is achieved by taking impression smears from the cut surface of liver and spleen (and often air sac membrane and peritoneum). These are fixed and stained with a modified acid-fast technique, and microscopic examination will then reveal typical 'inclusion bodies' of *Chlamydia* in infected cells. This procedure is fairly simple and quick and will give a 95 per cent confirmation of diagnosis. Final proof, however, depends on culturing the organism from the infected tissues, but this again takes time, and requires a very fresh carcase.

Apart from the problems that psittacosis causes in aviculture, a major consideration of this disease is that it is a zoonosis – that is to say it is transmissible to humans and will produce a severe and unpleasant illness, which is occasionally fatal. Symptoms are basically flu-like, with chest pains and breathing difficulties, weakness, headaches and fevers. Any person showing such signs, and who has had contact with birds, should always alert his medical practitioner of the possibility of psittacosis, which, in the human case, can be confirmed by a simple blood test. Treatment is usually rapidly successful with the use of tetracycline antibiotics.

Any bird keeper and veterinarian, faced with an outbreak of psittacosis, therefore has a difficult decision with regard to treatment and control. Spread of the disease within an avian population is rapid, mortality is high, and consideration must be taken of the human contacts, especially where children or people with respiratory difficulties are involved. Slaughter of infected birds, followed by thorough disinfection, should therefore be seriously considered as the right course of action.

Treatment is possible in selected cases, and should include isolation, thorough cleaning and disinfection, and the administration of chlortetracycline. This is best included in the feed, providing a more positive uptake than the common method of daily water medication, which allows rapid deterioration of the antibiotic. Severe, or single bird cases may be treated by injections of doxycycline. In any event, the treatment *must* be sustained for a minimum of 30, and preferably 45, days for any success to be achieved. The difficulties associated with the treatment of psittacosis are the variable and long incubation period, the prolonged medication required, the risk to humans involved during the process, and the fact that treated birds are immediately susceptible to reinfection once therapy ceases. Although measurable antibodies are produced in the blood, which can be used in diagnostic tests, these are not protective, and confer no immunity on the bird. Thus, if the environment is still contaminated with organisms, the bird will immediately reinfect once antibiotic therapy ceases.

In the UK psittacosis is not a notifiable disease, that is, public health authorities do not have to be involved in an outbreak, but any person connected with the infection in a bird should be aware of the potential serious damage to humans.

Loose Droppings

In the early part of this chapter it was pointed out that the droppings of a bird are a mix of both intestinal waste (faeces) and renal excretion (urine). In birds the latter is largely solid urate material, although there is a small proportion of actual liquid. The colour and appearance of the droppings produced can vary enormously, even in one individual, at different times and yet still be considered normal. The faecal content from a parrakeet is usually dark green, but will lighten if fruit or vegetable matter are consumed; the urine fraction is usually off-white. Droppings become more fluid if the bird is stressed or excited; those from egg-laying hens, or from any bird first thing in the morning, are much more copious than normal.

Loose droppings can be the result of an excessive urine fraction – polyuria – and will be a reflection of kidney or liver disease; or they can be the result of excessive watery faeces – diarrhoea – originating from an enteric disturbance. It is important to differentiate as to which fraction of the droppings is affected in order to make the correct diagnosis and institute suitable treatment.

Enteritis (Inflammation of the Bowel)

Enteritis can be caused by foreign irritants, such as coarse diet, excessive grit, chemicals, etc. and by stress factors, such as chilling, overcrowding, or change of diet, but most cases are infectious. Some viruses and fungi can be involved, and enteritis can be part of a more generalised disease, such as psittacosis, but most cases of bowel inflammation are caused by worms (see page 138), protozoa or bacteria.

Bacteria involved include *Pseudomonas*, *Pasteurella*, and *Salmonella* commonly, and many others occasionally, but probably the most frequent are *Escherichia coli* and *Yersinia pseudotuberculosis*. The former is a ubiquitious bacterium, found in the gut of most mammals and carnivorous birds, but, in common with other gram-negative bacteria, it is not normally found in seed- and grain-eating birds, such as the parrakeets. Infection is usually gained by contamination of food stuff by poor hygiene methods or from spoiling by rodents.

Affected birds will show the typical signs of illness – being ruffled, miserable, inappetant, etc., and passing liquid droppings of a pale colour. Specks of blood may be present. Treatment follows the usual course of isolation, warmth, oral fluids (if dehydration is severe, fluid therapy may be given parenterally) and soft food progressing to seed only, with the avoidance of fruit or green stuff, and antibiotic therapy, ideally as indicated by sensitivity testing.

137

Some cases may progress to a septicaemia – the *E. coli* organism passes from the gut to invade the body as a whole, and such birds usually die. *Post mortem* examination reveals an enteritis, but also an enlarged and congested liver, with cloudy air sacs and a greyish exudate on pericardial and air sac surfaces.

Yersinia pseudotuberculosis can manifest in an acute form, where birds are suddenly found dead with few warning signs, and *post mortem* examination reveals acute septicaemia. More usually, it is encountered in chronic form, where birds gradually lose weight, become lethargic and die. In these cases, autopsy shows multiple small focal abcesses in liver and spleen.

The organism is carried by wild birds and rodents, so the disease occurs in aviaries open to invasion by sparrows, mice and the like. Treatment is usually unsuccessful, so control depends upon hygiene and disinfection, and the security of the aviary against such outside invaders.

Internal Parasites

Internal parasites are of particular importance in parrakeets, and they include the roundworms (Nematodes) and tapeworms (Cestodes). Nematodes are of two broad types – the Ascarids, which are readily visible (up to 100–150 mm long and 2–3 mm in diameter); and the much finer Capillaria, or threadworms. These, as their name suggests, are like fine cotton threads. The treatment of these parasites has been well covered elsewhere in this book, but it is worth repeating that regular treatment (usually at six-monthly intervals) is essential, and that individual dosing is far more reliable and effective than blanket water medication.

Currently effective treatments are fenbenazole (Panacur) and Levamisole, although the latter appears to be more bitter-tasting.

Tapeworms are occasionally encountered and can be difficult to diagnose, unless segments are passed in the droppings, appearing as rice-grain-like objects. Affected birds will be generally unthrifty, and will sometimes have chronic diarrhoea. The treatment of choice is praziquantel (Droncit) which can be given either by injection, or as a crushed tablet, at the same dose rate as that recommended for small dogs.

Diseases of the Reproductive System

Male birds are rarely affected by such diseases, but hens can suffer from a number of important conditions.

During the breeding season the body of the hen undergoes considerable changes, as a result of hormonal influences, in order to produce her clutch of eggs. The ovary becomes considerably enlarged from its quiescent state, to produce follicles which release the ova. These pass down the developed oviduct and, during the journey, are coated with various layers of albumen, shell membranes, and eggshell, to produce the finished egg. The tubular oviduct becomes very enlarged and vascular, and may be ruptured, or the ovum may not be properly collected into the tube. This will result in an accumulation of high protein egg material in the abdominal cavity. The ensuing irritation, inflammation and infection is called 'egg peritonitis' and is usually rapidly fatal.

The production of eggshell requires considerable quantities of calcium, and if the hen's diet is deficient in this mineral, or if for some reason her body reserves cannot be mobilised adequately, she will then show signs of hypocalcaemia. This will manifest as thin-shelled eggs, smaller or reduced numbers of eggs, muscle weakness and bone 'softening', and difficulty in egg-laying, which can result in 'eggbinding'.

This problem has also been covered elsewhere, and can be caused by eggs which are too large or malformed, or by oviduct infection; but it is most usually the result of calcium deficiency resulting in reduced muscle activity in the oviduct. The egg then becomes lodged in the distal oviduct or the cloaca, and the bird rapidly weakens, becoming shocked and toxic. Apart from nursing care, such as lubrication, increased heat and humidity, and the administration of fluids as described, intramuscular calcium (with or without oxytocin) can often produce a rapid delivery, provided there is no physical obstruction, or prolapse of the oviduct.

Simple administration of calcium will not by itself correct a deficiency, as the body's utilisation of this mineral depends on the proper balance of calcium with phosphorus, and also the presence of Vitamin D3.

A commonly encountered problem in caged, rather than aviary, birds is the continued laying of eggs by a particular hen, with the result that enormous clutches are produced, and the bird becomes weakened by progressive loss of mineral and protein reserves.

Although progesterone-based hormones can be used to prevent this condition, a simpler and more natural technique is to reduce the photoperiod. Most cases arise because of the effect on the bird's 'internal clock' of prolonged daylight, making her feel as if she is in mid-summer. In households where people get up at six or seven in the morning, and are active in the evenings, until perhaps 11 pm, the bird in the living-room has an enforced day of 17 hours. By moving her to another room, or covering the cage at, say, 8 pm her day length is reduced to 14 hours, and egg-laying should cease.

Sexing

Many species of parrakeet are sexually dimorphic, that is to say that cock and hen can be distinguished by differences in external appearance, such as plumage colour and pattern. Others, however, are indistinguishable (monomorphic), or only attain their differences with maturity, such as the Indian Ringneck. For such birds various methods of determining sex have been devised to aid pairing and breeding programmes, without having to waste time waiting for nature to take its course.

The commonest and most widely used of these methods at present is so-called 'surgical sexing', a procedure that has been used for some years now. The gonads of a bird are internal, located at the anterior end of the kidneys, and these can be examined with a fibre-optic light source. The technique is well described in many avian publications, and usually requires a general anaesthetic, although some workers use only local anaesthesia. A trocar and cannula are passed through the left flank in the triangular space made by the last rib, the anterior muscle of the thigh, and the sternum, going through both skin and muscle layers. The trocar is then withdrawn, and the fibre-optic illuminated speculum is passed through the cannula. The magnified image of the internal anatomy allows easy inspection of the gonads. Male birds have paired, smooth, oval testes lying between the adrenal gland and the anterior pole of the kidneys. They will vary in size according to the age of the bird and the phase of the breeding cycle, but are usually pale cream to salmon pink in colour. In some species, such as the Crimson Rosella (Pennant), they are charcoal grey.

The ovary in parrakeets, in common with most bird species, is single, as only the left gonad develops (hence the operation is performed through the left flank). It is a more irregularly shaped organ than the testis, usually white to pale grey, with follicles imparting a caviar-like texture. The size of the follicles will vary considerably according to the phase of the breeding cycle.

This method has the advantage over other sexing techniques of being immediate, and also giving a precise picture of the health and activity of the gonads. It is at present far less expensive than other methods.

An alternative is faecal steroid testing, whereby the droppings are analysed for the presence of sex hormones. The procedure is difficult, expensive, and unreliable, as proportions of the hormones will vary with the time of year, and they will only be present in adult birds of breeding age. Surgical sexing can be carried out at any time of the year, and reliably on birds from four to five months old.

A newer alternative, which holds much promise for the future, is chromosome sexing. This technique requires the taking of a blood feather under hygienic conditions, and its transport in a special medium to a specifically equipped laboratory, where cells from the blood pulp are grown in cell culture. After about a week, growing cells are stained and examined under a microscope, where the dividing chromosomes can be identified, including those that determine sex.

At the time of writing this method has received widespread acceptance in the USA, but is only just developing in the UK. It is expensive, time-consuming, and more specialised than surgical sexing – it cannot give a cheap, immediate answer, nor can we tell anything about the condition of the gonads or the other internal organs. On the other hand, it can be carried out on any bird as soon as it has feathers – i.e. very young birds can be sexed by this method – and it is a non-invasive technique, so there is absolutely no risk to the bird involved.

Deficiency Diseases

Certain deficiencies in feeding can be a problem in parrakeets. Total nutritional deficiency – i.e. starvation – can be the result of ignorance or neglect on the part of the owner; or of difficulties experienced by the bird in taking food, caused perhaps by a damaged beak. In an aviary situation, a weaker bird may be prevented from feeding by its more dominant companions.

Some of the lesser minerals and B Vitamins may cause problems if deficient, but these are rarely seen in pure individual form except in experimental conditions, as most diets are adequate in these components. As exception would probably be a condition seen frequently in some of the smaller parrakeets, notably Turquoisines and Bourkes. The prominent symptom is 'torticollis' (twisted-neck), where the head is tilted to one side. There is an associated loss of balance and co-ordination. Many cases appear to be the result of damage to the nervous system due to lack of B Vitamins, and there seems also to be some failure in the bird's ability to utilise the vitamins fully, as the diet in most of these individuals appears to be adequate. Some inherited defect in absorption and utilisation may be involved, because I have seen a familial incidence in in-bred strains. Once the damage is done, birds seem unable to recover fully but administration of high doses of Vitamin B complex (parenterally if necessary) can prevent further outbreaks occurring.

An alternative reason for the same symptoms is an infection with *Listeria monocytogenes*, a bacterium which can cause sudden death with acute septicaemia, but, in its more chronic form, can also affect the nervous system to produce the same head tilt and loss of co-ordination. Once again, there is no cure once the balance is affected. Similar signs are seen with infection by Paramyxovirus and other neurotrophic viruses.

Calcium

Calcium deficiency is more common, either as a result of excessive demand during egg-laying or because of low intake. A bird eating a high seed diet will receive very little calcium, and the oil contained in the seed can, in some cases, reduce even further the bio-availability of that calcium by binding with it to form insoluble soaps.

Vitamin D

Vitamin D deficiency will result in rickets, which is a bowing deformity of the long bones of the legs, as a consequence of their failure to mineralise at their growing ends properly. This vitamin is closely linked with calcium metabolism, and the administration of Vitamin D3 and calcium will prevent or treat rickets in the early stages, although once the bones are severely bowed the deformity is irreversible.

Vitamin A

Vitamin A deficiency also occurs commonly, especially in birds fed a diet high in sunflower seed. As mentioned earlier, this vitamin is needed for the normal growth and integrity of epithelium, and its lack results in an excessive keratinisation and overgrowth of such tissues, with increased susceptibility to infection. Thick caseous plaques of yellow skin debris may be found in such areas as mouth and throat, and the bird is more likely to have such problems as conjunctivitis and candidiasis.

Other vitamin and mineral deficiencies are rarely encountered in these birds.

Drugs and Dosages

There is little virtue in listing recommended drugs and their dose rates, as such a list would be out of date even before it was printed. The pet-bird market is not of great interest to commercial drug companies, so very few medicaments are produced specifically for cage and aviary birds. This is in marked contrast to the large market for commercially important flocks, such as poultry, game birds and pigeons. Most drugs in common usage on pet birds, therefore, are those produced originally for use in flock birds, dogs and cats, or even humans, which, by trial and error in the hands of interested veterinary surgeons and aviculturists, have proved useful and efficient.

The range of such drugs is expanding rapidly, as interest in avian medicine develops, and new products are continually being described as being effective in birds. Lists of the more commonly used drugs are readily available in existing publications on avian medicine: one particularly useful volume in the UK is *Avian Medicine and Surgery* by Brian Coles. The serious practitioner is recommended to keep up to date with rapid advances by reading journals and periodicals relating to avian treatment.

A few general comments are worth noting: prolonged antibiotic therapy, especially with broad-spectrum drugs, can seriously affect the normal flora of the gut, so an intermittent treatment regime may be used. Alternatively, replacement therapy with natural yogurt, or products such as Transvite or Canaddase may be considered.

Preparations of tetracyclines are not well absorbed from the gut in the presence of calcium ions, so the administration of calcium supplements simultaneously with these antibiotics, is counterproductive.

Injectable treatment of sick birds is of great value, but it is worth remembering that the injection of a volume as small as 0.1 ml into a small bird, weighing perhaps 100 gm, is equivalent to giving 25 ml to a 25 kg dog. Therefore, administration must be careful, especially when the bird is debilitated and the muscle mass available is much reduced.

It is hoped that this chapter has given some insight into the disease problems of these very popular and attractive birds, and that enthusiasts may be pointed in the right direction for nursing and treatment techniques, should their birds begin to show signs of illness or distress.

Useful Addresses

UK

The Avicultural Society The Secretary, Warren Hill, Halford's Lane, Hartley Wintney, Hampshire RG27 8AG (quarterly magazine).

Bird Keeper Prospect House, 9–13 Ewell Road, Cheam, Sutton, Surrey SM1 4QQ (new colour magazine for aviculturists, launched in June/July 1988).

Cage and Aviary Birds Prospect House, 9–13 Ewell Road, Cheam, Surrey SM1 4QQ: 06–661–4491 (weekly magazine).

Data Bird Worldwide Ltd The Willows, Denton, Peterborough PE7 38D: 0733–242714.

The European Aviculture Council Dave Axtell, PO Box, 74 Bury St Edmunds, Suffolk (an organisation formed to protect the rights of bird keepers in the UK and in Europe; membership open to all bird keepers).

Gloucester Laboratories (Veterinary) Ltd, St Oswald's Road, Cattle Market, Gloucester GL1 29J: 0452–24961; (*post mortem* service).

Interlink, Portland House, 22–24 Portland Square, Bristol BS2 8RZ: 0272–40257.

Ministry of Agriculture and Fisheries Animal Health Office, Belfast, Northern Ireland (0232–650111 ext. 289) (for export and import licences for Northern Ireland).

Ministry of Agriculture and Fisheries Animal Health Divisional Headquarters, Governmental Buildings, Hook Rise, Tolworth, Surrey: 01–337–6611 (for export and import licences).

Ministry of Environment Headquarters Buildings, Tolworth Towers, Surbiton, Surrey: 01–399–5191 (for export and import licences).

National Council for Aviculture Secretary, 87 Winn Road, Lee, London SE12 9EY. (Membership open to all bird keepers – helps to protect all the rights of bird keepers.)

Oaklands Park Farm Aviaries Paul and June Bailey, Newdigate, Nr Dorking, Surrey: 029–384–408 (commercial establishment selling birds, aviaries, cages, seeds, accessories and all equipment).

Southern Aviaries Max Sanderson, Brook House Farm, Tinker's Lane, Hadlow Down, Nr Uckfield, East Sussex: 082–585–283 (commercial establishment selling all equipment for birds).

USA

American Federation of Aviculture (AFA) PO Box 1568, Nedondo Beach, California 90278 (bi-monthly magazines dealing with all aspects of aviculture).

The National Parrot Association 8NO, Hoffman Lane, Hauppauge, N.Y. 11788 (bi-monthly magazine, dedicated to the care and protection of parrots).

Australia

The Avicultural Society of Australia c/o Graeme Hyde, 52 Harris Road, Elliminyt, Victoria 3249.

New Zealand

Avicultural Society of N.Z. (Inc) Roy Fitch, Editor *Foreign Birds*, P.O. Box 21, 403 Henderson, Auckland.

Canada

The British Columbia Avicultural Society Val Parry, Box 2091, New West BC, V3L 5A3.

The Parrot Club of Manitoba D. Chimda, 1145 Manitoba Avenue, Winnipeg, Manitoba, REX OK6.

Singapore

Singapore Avicultural Society The Secretary, 6 Chapel Road, Singapore 1542.

Bibliography

Ahyone, J., on Lutino Adelaide, AFA *Watchbird*, Vol XII, No. 1, Feb/
March 1985, p. 4

Baker, Dr J., on management, *Cage and Aviary Birds*, 30 Jan 1988

Boosey, E.J., on *Psittacula*, *Foreign Bird Keeping*, Ilife Books, 1956

Bringas, R., on Princess of Wales, AFA *Watchbird*, Vol. XLV, No. 3,
June/July 1987, pp. 51–53

Cole, B.H., *Avian Medicine and Surgery*, Blackwell Scientific Publications,
1985

Dingle, S., on *Psittacula* Ringnecks, AFA *Watchbird*, Vol. XIII, No. 5,
Oct/Nov 1986, p. 24

Erhart, R., on *Neophemas*, AFA *Watchbird*, Vol. IX, No. 1, Feb/March 1982

Forshaw, J., *Australian Parrots*, second edition, Lansdowne Editions,
1981

Forshaw, J., *Parrots of the World*, TFH, 1978

Hayward, J., on *Psephotus*, *Cage and Aviary Birds*, 16 Jan 1988

Hutchins, B.R. and Lovell, R.H., *Australian Parrots, A Field and Aviary
Study*, revised edition, Avicultural Society of Australia

Low, R., *Parrots, Their Care and Breeding*, second edition, Blandford
Press, 1986

Mandeville, M., on *Psittacula*, Parrot Society magazine, No. XXL, July
1987

Parrot Society Breeding Register 1984 (*Neophemas*); 1985 (*Psittacula*)

Phipps, G., on Kakarikis, AFA *Watchbird*, Vol. X, No. 1, Feb/March 1983

Smith G., *Lovebirds and Related Parrots*, Paul Elek Ltd, 1979

Zomer, H.P.M., *Neophemas en hun Kleumaties (Neophemas and their Mutations)*, Arnhem, 1987

Index